Some Answers Without Questions

LAVINIA GREENLAW

Some
Answers
Without
Questions

faber

First published in 2021
by Faber & Faber Limited
Bloomsbury House
74–77 Great Russell Street
London WC1B 3DA

Typeset by Faber & Faber Limited
Printed and bound by CPI Group (UK) Ltd, Croydon, CR0 4YY

A CIP record for this book
is available from the British Library

ISBN 978–0–571–36865–5

10 9 8 7 6 5 4 3 2 1

For my mother when she was Lindsay Mackintosh
For my great-grandmother when she was Alice Ballard
For my nain when she was Doris Elaine Griffith-Jones
For Ethel Butler

. . . 'Where does the thunder sleep?
Where doth he hide his terrible head? And his swift and fiery
daughters,
Where do they shroud their fiery wings, and the terrors of
their hair?'

William Blake, 'Tiriel'

A word about the weather
There is no weather per se in this book. Passing reference is
made to weather in a few instances. Assume whatever season
you like throughout. Summer makes the most sense in a book
of this length. That way, pages do not have to be used up
describing people taking off and putting on overcoats.

Fran Ross, *Oreo*

Contents

III

1. I wasn't there

At fifteen, I suffered a rupture that I still can't explain. My mother later described it as *When you stopped being able to learn.* My mind locked away what it knew and refused to absorb anything further so that I started to fail at school in subjects where I'd not had to try. At this time I was putting most of my energy into having feelings – reading and writing poems, listening to music, falling in and out of love, going anywhere and doing anything in hope of experience. No wonder I found this sudden blankness restful. It was so absolute that I didn't really understand it was happening and did not ask for help.

By then I knew something of the dangers of presence and what it might attract. If I put myself forward to be seen or heard, I was inviting a response. If the bad thing happened, it was my fault because I had been dancing or drinking or walking in the woods. I had raised my hand or laughed or argued back. I had opened a door and entered a room. I had seen and heard. My presence was the explanation for whatever happened next. So perhaps I was refusing to be present or refusing to learn more about this.

Or the rupture was the result of some internal equation: opposing forces cancelling each other out. I was afraid of agency but determined on experience, guarded and avid, brimming and shrinking. Despite this, I wanted to be there – wherever there was – so badly that I overcame the fear of negotiating a world in which I had stopped working. This was also a time when everything felt important, above all who I was standing next to, what I was listening to, what I wore and said, and how I moved and all I felt. I was so intensely there that I could not bear it.

When I was forty, I began work on a book about the role music can play in growing up. I was the single mother of a teenager. I'd escaped a bad situation, secured us a home, published three books and had started to teach. I'd been discussed and reviewed, praised, rewarded, criticised and rejected, and I thought I had the good and bad of all that at a healthy remove. Life was more rewarding and calmer than it had ever been. Yet I could not bring myself to break a habit I didn't even know I had: that I would withhold myself rather than risk presence. On page 192 I left home, and on page 193 I had a baby. In the years between those two pages I sang in a band and made a record but I knew, from the start, that I wasn't going to mention any of this. People ask why and I haven't known what to say. The decision occurred at such a deep level that I'm not even aware of having made it. Now I'm in my late fifties and almost as far from that forty-year-old as she was from the teenager she wrote about. I've been wondering about that silence and why, in a book about music, I withheld the one time I made it the focus of my life. Between eighteen and twenty I was at college but I also did this other thing. A handful of people thought of me as a singer. I sang.

Writing the book took me back to the record shop where I used to hang out after class, wanting to talk about music and relieved to have found others to whom it meant so much. I was

4

as intent as all the other people in the room, who were boys. Their expertise was nuanced, judgemental and competitive – mine too. I kept turning up at the shop until someone said hello and then the man behind the counter knew my name and held things back that he thought I'd like and we became friends. He was always interested in what I had to say but, on the whole, the boys were just waiting for their turn to speak.

We didn't document our lives and had few photographs to share. We just said, *I was there*. This meant more than that you'd turned up. It suggested that you were part of a scene. Much of the talk was about having been at a particular concert, one that had already been deemed legendary. Anyone could listen to a record but being in the room, even knowing how to find it, meant that you were *serious*. Even now when I say I like a particular band, a man will ask only if I saw them, when and where. He will then give a tight nod and ask nothing further because he's not interested in my thoughts about the band so much as whether or not I have the right to talk about them. The concerts I went to are all in my diary but even so I wonder if I'm making it up. So much of me wasn't there at all.

I remember two versions of myself in that shop. There was the one who trusted her knowledge and taste, and who held fierce opinions, and who made her way into the group by persisting. I made myself present. *I'm still here.* But there was also the one who would silence herself and diminish her own presence so as to be allowed to remain. *I'm not really here.* How did I expect to claim anyone's attention when I was barely present? I wanted to say this and this and this but to step aside as I said it.

5

This movement between presence and absence might be a failure of nerve but it is also key to how I write. I start by being intensely present and work towards my own disappearance, which can be achieved even when writing in the first person. The idea is *Look at this* not *Look at me*. I use myself in order to articulate an experience that can be recognised by someone I've never met. I have to step aside so that they can point at the page and say to themselves *Look at me*.

Since I was first published thirty years ago, I've been asked questions about writing, and about myself, that I haven't wanted to answer. I've been so strongly conditioned to respond that even when the question is hostile or intrusive, I usually try. *It's only polite*. The person who asks the question controls what is discussed. Where my closest friends might hesitate to enquire, strangers give themselves permission, and I hand over my private self. Questions about writing can be just as tricky as the personal ones because they're often far too general to address or aren't questions at all but someone making a point. Still I do my best, rushing around, gathering detail, doubling back. I am driven to be precise (*to tell the truth*) and so say a bit more and usually too much. When I'm seen, I want to be seen clearly – who doesn't? I'm quite relaxed about what people see in my work but I do not want them to tell me who I am.

These days I find it easier to deflect a question and I am anyway more interested in what might lie behind it – the assumptions out of which the question has been formed. I try to question the question or to say what feels most true without shaping this to what I'm being asked. I have started to think

6

about what I have never been asked – the answers without questions, the unframed response.

The questions I'm asked remain those of the investigative precept: What do you write about? Where do you write? When do you write? Why do you write? The only question missing is Who. Who is writing this?

My voice arose out of the desire to connect and was shaped in reaction and resistance. It became my own when I started to use words in a way for which I had no example. All the voices I used to imitate, knowingly or not, fell silent and the only one I could hear was my own. And who likes the sound of their own voice?

This process is enacted again and again as my voice changes and I approach a new book. Each time, it feels as if I've stopped working. Something in me is saying no but in doing this it is setting out towards what it wants to say yes to. Perhaps this is what happened when I was fifteen.

2. Notes on anger

I am angry and much of my anger is directed towards myself. For not saying that I didn't agree and didn't want, not that, not now, not there, and stop and no. For, in the largest and smallest situations, letting others decide what I intended because I could not bring myself to resist, let alone correct them.

For a long time I was afraid of this anger and worried that if I paid it direct attention, it would overwhelm what I wanted to think and write about. I've come to believe that it defines me – not the anger itself but the force it moves to protect. Because although I wasn't speaking up, I was taking note. I saw and knew and remembered even if I didn't act accordingly.

A man I loved when I was young scribbled a quote from Nietzsche on a slip of paper and gave it to me. I was enchanted by this man and read the quote he gave me as a spell, one I could recite without any real consideration.

> The great periods of our life occur when we gain the courage to rechristen what is bad about us as what is best.[1]

You can find it scattered all over the internet like breadcrumbs, a fairy-tale solution *Follow this*. I was desperate for someone to scatter breadcrumbs, and followed the man without looking where I was going just as I followed Nietzsche's advice without thinking about what it might mean. Now I'm starting to understand what rechristening entails. Not a quick fix through renaming things or a shuffle of interpretation that tells you everything's fine, but that sometimes you get to a point where all you can do is face the dark parts, they're all you have left, and so you turn them over. You don't transform yourself or rename the dark parts but you look clearly at their powers and make use of them.

There was the discovery that what I felt was anger and then the recognition of anger as a reasonable response. After that there were the years of plain anger when I was ashamed and afraid of myself. Now my anger seems to have revealed its opposite nature as a form of power, an electrification.

Anger sustains me – as long as I do not get angry. Anger needs to be described.

Becoming angry is a form of perceptual collapse. It's an obliteration, not an assertion, of the self. I sound as if I'm attacking what's around me when really I'm just trying to hold my place. My anger is often about the failure of someone to hear what I'm saying, which of course to me is clear and logical and why wouldn't anyone respond with *That makes sense! Let me revise and build on that!* But I am not clear and logical. I'm desperate and my language, too, has collapsed – *fuck . . . fucking . . . fuck.* Whenever I hear someone else, particularly a woman, swearing like this, I wince because it will be perceived as a loss of control and so a loss of authority. To express anger that will be taken seriously, you have to sound not angry at all. You must speak in measured tones, calmly and coherently and without evident bias. But isn't anger a response to what seems unbalanced, dishonest, unfair?

Anger, when delivered with total conviction, can hold its authority. I have felt anger billow out of me to no effect because the other person has been able to tell that I am willing to deny it. But anger is a form of energy. Trapped, it concentrates. It loses its hold on its subject or target and reverses itself.

Anger might be a form of power but it is the body's last resort. It becomes a first resort in situations that repeat themselves.

In childhood, I could make a lot of noise that sounded angry but I experienced this noise only as a loss of control, as desperation, a plea. I wanted the person I was angry with to love and hold me. They didn't need to agree with me but I desperately wanted them to understand. I never thought of that feeling as justified, assertive or clear.

I learnt to express fear in the form of a question and while that question might have been addressed, no one addressed my fear.

There is something unbreachable about a lie told with total conviction. Even when you brandish the proof, if the liar holds their nerve, your righteous outrage falters. You have been trained to be *reasonable* and to *see both sides*. You scurry from one side to the other till you have no idea where you are. The liar remains absolutely still. You become a blur and they are terribly clear. Their refusal of fact and evidence and reason is dazzling. You take your anger back inside yourself but no longer trust it. Are you mad?

I was angry because although I knew it was a lie, I believed it. I let the lie lie.

The last time I was extremely angry, I said things that I regretted because they were unkind – but none of them were untrue. I meant what I said. The blurting of them so shocked me that I had to examine them afterwards. They weren't resolved but they had been ejected and externalised, and so could now be seen and grasped. I moved to conceal them again but, to my astonishment, stopped myself. I meant what I said.

I have never chosen to raise my voice in anger. It happens without volition and as a result of words being shoved (shovelled, even) out of my mouth and into the air by my smallest self. I am doing what I can to push back or to stay put. I am also, disastrously, reaching out.

Children suffer the anger of parents who shout when they are tired or in pain or miss a bus or drop a cup or cannot turn on a machine. Later they take the child in their arms and say, *I'm sorry I shouted, I had a terrible day*, and believe they have deleted any harm. Perhaps they have.

11

A child doesn't have the manoeuvres, the sentences. Their anger is pure and red and quick and easily dismissed.

If a parent is never angry then a child has no model for anger. When it arises within themselves, they might experience it as an illness, a visitation of something foreign and hostile that needs to be expelled, and it does seem to move outwards, and to pass, only to turn up again. It is gone and not gone, like a haunting.

Before I was old enough to moderate my anger, I would say the terrible thing and nothing happened. That was more disturbing than a response.

Anger can be withheld to the point where it becomes constituent: no longer an emotion but a texture deep in the tissue.

My idea of being is one of capacity – what I'm able to contain rather than what I might take in. There is little choice in what is taken in. Anger can be the only way to say *Enough*.

It is easy to be angry on someone else's behalf because your role is to convey rather than to express.

Why, when my own anger seems impotent, am I so afraid of the anger of others? If I hold my ground or press or say no, I am overwhelmed by fear. Each act of assertion, anything I know might disappoint or provoke, prompts dread to the extent that I avoid the response. I'm afraid to read the most routine message because of the anger it might contain. When you can't hear someone's voice, anger is easy to construe. You can deflect it by refusing to listen.

I live in a time of reduced gestures, where words and actions are abbreviated, and the barely perceptible act of hostility gathers power. The more it is cloaked in light conversation, the harder it is to deflect. There are people who, whenever I meet them, offer something of this kind. They smile as they say it and I smile back, even murmuring agreement. I try to work out what they want (what will make them go away). I'm paralysed by a detonation in my body, something like a depth charge, which feels so internal that it has to be of my own making. If I recognised it as anger, I might be able to act.

You're better at talking about feelings than feeling them. Although my talking about feelings quickly becomes noise, I still try to feel in words. It seems the clearest way to make sense of myself and to convey what I want to. I realise now that going straight to words can be a way to reach past myself. It is possible that I use words to disown myself. Why, then, am I surprised when others fail to see me?

It doesn't always help to tell. If I made a list now of the events that make me most angry with myself, I would not stop feeling that anger.

The point is not to defuse the past but to defuse myself and the way to do that is to become more angry, to allow that anger is

13

assertion, insistence, and needs to move rather than be met.

I followed the man in the fairy tale into the forest where he rechristened everything about me. By the time he'd finished, I was the forest. *Why have you brought me here?* he said. He had such conviction in his anger that he didn't need to raise his voice. Even in this I followed him and so turned on myself. *Why have you brought me here?* I said.

3. The noise I learnt to make as a young animal

My first winter was one of tremendous snow. It started to fall in London on Boxing Day and didn't thaw until March. For those three months, there was not a single night without frost. The Thames iced over and the sea froze a mile from shore.

My mother was twenty-five and I was the second of her four children, all born twenty months apart. She put me and my brother in the pram, stowed the washing underneath and on top of us, and inched her way down the hill to the launderette. The pavement was packed with snow and snow rose in great walls to either side. She had to push everything back up the hill too. She made coal fires and filled paraffin heaters, and kept us well wrapped up. She had no access to thermal underwear or down jackets. It was simply a matter of adding more layers. Our beds were made up of sheets and blankets, and so she added more blankets. Day and night, we were packed in wool.

Frost gripped the windows and in the morning the inside of the glass dripped with the liquid of our cooled breath. Milk bottles put out at the end of the day sank beneath more snow by morning. Cars, animals and people were disappearing. Our bodies concentrated on keeping warm and we gathered ourselves inwards. Everything slowed – all movement from the blood in our veins to the birds in the sky. Imagine the hush, the peace, the danger.

At five months, I was starting to look about me. My first idea of the world was of a palpable emptiness with which I had no direct contact. I should have been developing a sense of distance, colour, surface and depth but I was moved around a blank geometry, across white planes and between white walls. As I began to see further, these shapes grew no clearer. My place in the world would always be unanchored, my vision a rush towards emptiness, my approaches out of kilter – too much, too little, too late, too soon.

I woke each day beside a window with a view onto a freshly undisturbed garden but beyond that, the snow was less simple. As the weeks passed, the tremendous dishevelled piles that lined the roads exuded black, grey, yellow and brown as if leaching the true colours of the city from what lay beneath.

I had been born at home on the hill on a grey summer afternoon. Four weeks earlier, smog had blanketed the city. London was still a place of gas, steam and coal, its air heavy with particulates. Its streets were jagged with demolition and bomb sites, and the towers of Westminster looked as if they were built out of soot. When the smog returned again in December, I was mostly asleep. I could grasp what my mother passed to me but I didn't yet know how to let it go.

The sounds I heard were minor: the relaxing hiss of the par-affin heater, the muttering of coal, the wheels of the pram, the clump of boots, my mother's voice in continual murmur and play. She has a lovely voice, rather like a fall of snow, and she sang to me. Imagine the quiet of a home where there is only the telephone, the doorbell and the radio. I didn't cry often. Kept close to my mother, in that quiet world, I didn't need to.

I was eight months old before the earth revealed itself. No wonder I was so eager to explore it. *The first time I let you crawl across the garden, I had to take a dead wasp and a rusty nail out of your mouth.* That summer, my mother was pregnant again with my sister and I started to make noise.

Of course I remember nothing of this. All I know is what I feel when that winter is described, which is complicit, austere, held and at peace. A still world of deep snow and darkness restored me forty years later when I travelled north of the Arctic Circle in midwinter. Each day there was a brief time of pallid, primordial light but otherwise I was in darkness. The temperature dropped to minus fifty and I disappeared under layers of clothes. Movement and speech were such an effort that my mind slowed down too. My need to formulate the world, always so urgent, gave way and my thoughts relaxed. I started to make notes towards a different kind of poetry that would be less crowded and eventful. I wanted to look rather than feel, to stay still, and to spend more time in the dark.

The noise I learnt to make as a young animal is lightly substanced – like salt, snow or grit. Its arrangements are crystalline. It is a series of minor gestures with an underlying precariousness, a testing of surfaces, the taking of small steps, an acceptance of blanks, an urge to get lost, a tension around form. A distaste for signs, directions, swift movement and sudden change. It can be stiff, anxious, layered, fulfilled, insular, intimate and withdrawn.

All my life I have dreamt of going to sleep in snow. This is not about imposing myself on emptiness. Not even an empty page is empty. Whatever it is – snow or page – I want to dissolve into it, to be so present that I'm no longer there.

4. Lalage

The first words a child utters are greeted with delight but sooner or later people will tell them to stop talking. They are instructed to wait, to be quiet, not to interrupt, not to complain. Language can no longer be used for its own sake. Now it has to be organised, selected and timed.

Once I discovered my voice I didn't stop talking, even before I could use words. So young that I couldn't yet cross a room of my own volition, I dispersed great plumes of language that were almost entirely sound. I babbled out of joy. I wanted to respond to the world, to join in. When a visitor appeared, I pulled myself up in my cot and was as voluble as I was incomprehensible. *You put all you had into communicating welcome.*

I grew into a creature who looked outwards from a body I understood (if at all) as electricity or weather. My imperatives were acute and I struggled with containment. I did not apply words to myself and so my aspects and processes had no form. My voice was a way for thoughts and feelings to leave my body, and a way to manage atmosphere. I see myself in those children who pick up on tension and can't stop talking. It's as if they're compelled to keep offering words in the hope that they might hit on the ones that need to be said.

My father nicknamed me Lalage, explaining that she was a young girl who didn't stop talking. Not couldn't but didn't. I was confused because he was smiling as he said this but how could it not be a complaint? I now think he was smiling because he was pleased with himself. He had made a literary joke. In that moment, my father prompted a hesitation. I now knew there was such a thing as talking too much.

Lalage appears briefly in Horace's poem '*Integer Vitae*' to illustrate a point about love. She is not only too young to be wooed but too talkative. How can any man address her if she doesn't shut up? Unlike Scheherazade, a genius architect who builds as she speaks, Lalage babbles. This is also translated as prattling, which isn't as urgent or as fluid but just as annoying. Her voice is shapeless. She speaks constantly and her sentences are so overcrowded that her words barely have room to form. She's talking her way out of a dangerous situation as her babbling asserts her child state. Horace[2] advises that this 'sweet-talking' child is too young to bear the weight of desire, using the blunt image of an animal being put to the yoke. Subjected to sexual attention, she would lower her head. Her voice would be cut off.

Lalage's babble allows her to keep others at a distance while continuing to assert her presence. The words that pour out of her are an alternative form of substance. They say that she is here and cannot be ignored and also that she is intractable. They are meaningless, unmeasurable and ill-timed, and as such they remain her own.

A lot of my talking as a child was the saying out loud of thoughts that I wanted to fix and couldn't yet write down. When alone, I told myself stories and spun rhymes without being aware that I was actually speaking. I had no thought of being heard. Talking to yourself is a form of speech that bypasses the need for connection. It completes itself.

My father wanted me to talk and to know poetry but neither more than he did. For a long time, a love of books was our bond. One day it seemed I had read past him and then my writing went from being a child's inventiveness to words on a page. When I told him I was going to have a book published he said, *Your little brother used to write poetry, what a pity he stopped.* There's a photograph of my father that breaks my heart. He is so serious and young, clutching a book in one hand and a pipe in the other. Perhaps he was telling me that he used to write poetry. I never thought to ask.

My books became another way that the world was telling him he wasn't good enough. After he died, I found a file in his study that contained clippings of dozens of reviews and interviews about my work. When the internet took over, he had printed them off. I regularly meet people who say how proud he was of me, which the family noticed he could not say to my face. *Apparently I don't tell you how proud of you I am, well I am.* He was rigid with effort as he said this and I was too young to understand the place this difficulty came from.

—

There was a time in my adult life when I started to talk to myself again. It was not a consequence of being alone but of being unheard. I accompanied myself around the house, along the aisles in the supermarket, across the street, and up and down the stairs. *You have no idea what it's like to live with someone who talks to themselves all the time.* I was surprised because the man who said this seemed unable to tell when I was not talking to him. *What? What did you say?* Only then would I realise that I had spoken out loud. Or maybe he could tell but was insisting that if he was in the room, I should be there with him. He was tugging me back from the place he referred to as *your interior world*, which he spoke of as *rich and deep*, as if these were troubling qualities for an interior world to have. He was saying that I wasn't there. I didn't understand the difficulty.

The movement between presence and absence – which I've described as a failure of substance and a refusal to connect but also as how I form my writing and myself – is neither simple nor stable nor consistent. I am unaware of it happening and so have given little thought to its impact on those around me. I don't really talk about, let alone share, my writing (*How was your day?*) but I don't really stop working either. The process of gathering, forming and arranging is continuous, so much so that I can't conceive of it as separate to myself. Therefore, to me, it isn't happening and I don't realise how absent I might appear.

In writing, I'm subsiding into a professionalised daydream. It is my work and not something from which I ever fully emerge. First I learnt not to talk about it because others might be bored or alarmed, and then I discovered that I wanted, and needed, to keep my words to myself. If you share your words too quickly, they don't have the chance to gather their true meaning. If, like Lalage, you babble and prattle, you are only making noise.

5. Being good with words

You hardly needed to learn to read and write: they were just there.

I was often told that I was *good with words* and it never sounded like a compliment. Children can straightforwardly excel at dance, athletics, art or maths but a kid like me, who sat in the library reading *The Odyssey* during lunch break and described an author's prose style as *idiosyncratic*, prompts unease. This scrappy ten-year-old was giving a bad performance of being a grown-up. It wasn't *natural*. It would be fine for her to win a spelling competition, which is after all a kind of sport. But when she brandished words that had been placed out of reach and appeared to know what they mean, it was as if she had picked up a sword. She was not to be trusted with such things. Not yet.

Of course words are a weapon but they are an unreliable one. Who knows exactly where they will land and what blow they will deliver? They are unstable too. The over-articulate child is trying to be clear and so why do her words, meant to turn on lights and open windows, just hang there? It's as if she is speaking in heavy furniture.

I couldn't get over the discovery that while words were just air, what I built out of them seemed as real as anything else, if not more so. The surging worlds in my head could be given form as stories or poems. I could walk among them. I was the child who found such joy in articulation that when a teacher asked the class a question, they would sometimes pretend not to see my raised hand. I wasn't trying to show off. That would have required more social awareness than I had at the time. When I used the word *idiosyncratic*, the teacher told me to stand up. Stone-faced, she asked if I knew what it meant. I gave an explanation and was told to sit down. She'd been confident that I didn't know and the fact that I did made me no more popular with her or anyone else. Another teacher told me that I was precocious, enjoying the fact that this was a word I didn't know. He explained it not as clever but *clever-clever . . . and no one likes a girl who is that*. If I were to be truly good with words, I had to learn when not to use them.

At first I let the words flow and then I started to say as much as I could in as few words as possible. It took a long time to learn that concision can be like a block of powder paint and sometimes you need to add water. I also wanted to say something as quickly as possible and get out of there. I was still worrying about the dangers of being present and was unnerved by the substance of what I produced. When I wrote my first novel and was handling tens of thousands of words, I stopped being able to spell. I was no longer sure of the correct way to use apostrophes or commas. I had seen too many words.

—

Living in books has meant locating myself by writers and London is full of them. It is particularly crowded with dead men. I was born in a house built by Evelyn Waugh's father. Keats House is next to the library that I used as a child. Rimbaud slapped Verlaine with a fish near the pool where I learnt to swim. Now I live between Isaac Rosenberg and Louis Mac-Neice, and not far from the home of Edmund Gosse. Born in 1849 and brought up within the Plymouth Brethren, Gosse was given only religious texts to read and taught to receive them as fact. His father was a zoologist who struggled to protect his beliefs against emerging theories of evolution. Gosse used to escape to the attic.

> The garret was a fairy place. It was a low lean-to, lighted from the roof. It was wholly unfurnished except for two objects, an ancient hat-box and a still more ancient skin-trunk.[3]

This loosely made, undomesticated space with its two un-explained boxes offered the child freedom and mystery. When his father explained that one was a hat-box, the boy tried to wear it on his head as if insisting it make sense of itself. After all, words meant exactly what they said. The trunk turned out to be empty but it was lined with pages from a sensational novel. Gosse had no idea what a novel was because 'the idea of fiction, of a deliberately invented story, had been kept from me with entire success'. He believed that the story of the lady flee-ing her country to escape villainous rogues was a true account, and started to worry about his mother whenever she went out. The story broke off in the middle of one of its most exciting sentences, which, he says, 'wound me up almost to a disorder of wonder and romance'.[4] His father must have hoped that the Bible would fill him with wonder but how could it if every-thing it described simply happened?

The excitement of the story lining the trunk was all the more

24

intense for the boy because he did not know how to process it. He'd never before had the experience of being drawn into a scene that was not supposed to convince him of itself but rather to activate something within him. The incompleteness of this fragment, the sudden suspension of narrative, would also have introduced him to the pleasures of suspense. Gosse became very good with words and went on to be a poet, critic, translator and all-round man of letters. He wrote a defence of 'exotic forms' in poetry, championed the villanelle and translated Ibsen. Perhaps he sought out the ways in which language might confound him in the hopes of a little more wonder and romance.

—

I lived in books to the extent that most of the time I was elsewhere: Narnia, Wonderland, Neverland, Ancient Greece, Zanzibar, Samarkand, a French cheese factory, an American prairie, a chalet in the Swiss Alps, the South Pole, the moon. I made no distinction between the actual and the imagined. Given I hadn't been anywhere, they were all equally plausible. I didn't leave my own island for the first ten years of my life. On maps, its size was routinely exaggerated but I knew that I came from a small place. For holidays, we travelled south or west to its edge and watched the horizon as if the great elsewhere were about to float into view.

My first crush, at ten, was on a boy in my class who came from Mauritius. I pored over the map, thrilled by how far away it was from here, and how, unlike Britain, it looked like a proper island in a proper sea. He had a musical name, which I still sometimes sing to myself, but he was also so delightful that I've had to stop myself measuring every man against him since. He remains, for me, the ideal man and Mauritius, where I've never been, the ideal island.

For all that I long to be elsewhere, I'm not much good at being on holiday. I was recently in Greece when one of the teenagers came across me sitting in the shade with my notebook. She asked, pityingly, *Do you have to write?* It took me back to my first foreign holiday at the age of ten, when we borrowed someone's dilapidated villa in Menorca. For all the excitement of flying, the dazzle and blue water, the lizards and ruined stone and living by lamplight, what captivated me was language. I found a parallel-text anthology of Spanish poetry and a dictionary, and set about making translations. No one minded and nor were they interested. Wherever we went, I found books and disappeared into them. If anything I was considered eccentric and was accommodated as long as I didn't bore on.

Writing began as a way of translating the world and locating myself within it. Later, it became a form of reply. It is not an overstatement to say that being able to write has made sense of my life as well as of myself and I feel endlessly fortunate about that. I'm never at a loss for something to do, I've never thought about who to be, and I could never not do or be this. So yes, I have to.

6. The act of writing

From the start, writing took place in a separate dimension. I was barely aware of what I'd done. People asked what I wanted to be when I grew up and I never knew quite what to say. I didn't aspire to be a writer because writing was something I already did. When I was about eight, a teacher told me that I'd won a prize for an essay I'd written about my tortoise, and my first thought was *Did I write an essay about my tortoise?* I still don't remember the actual writing part of writing. When it's working, all conscious aspects – ideas, technique – synthesise and cannot be detected. It's like learning a dance or a language, taking it step by step and then suddenly feeling the thing flow.

You used to read and write in bed after lights out, with a torch or a dimmed bedside lamp. I pretended not to know, and so didn't ask or look for anything. But you were tired, of course. My mother's tact was so absolute that it never occurred to me that someone might be aware of what I was doing. I had the luxury of space and time in which I was not overlooked. I still write best in or on a bed. My body likes to be arranged in a way that my mind associates with letting slip. I could never work in a café, though I can write quite easily on buses and trains. This has grown harder since notebooks became an accessory and I realised that people were judging me. *Who does she think she is?* Before that they would have thought, if anything, that I just needed to write something down.

27

My first notebook was given to me by a friend when I was eighteen and it prompted me to document my thoughts and gather the things I wrote. It was an artist's sketchbook with a plain black cover and blank pages, about the size of a paperback. I've varied this format over the years but always come back to it. I don't write, or think, in sequence, and I use the page as open space, drawing diagrams and sketches. Ruled lines would impose organisation before my thoughts are ready for that. I've worked in notebooks that I didn't like because they were cheap or a gift or the only thing available. I was also making a point to myself about not over-investing in the words I produced. When I lived in Massachusetts in the nineties, I first encountered the notebook as object. Does anyone really believe that if they write on pages containing gold thread or pressed leaves their words will emerge golden and pressed? You need to be able to make a mess of a page and how can you do that when the page is so expensive?

This was in Amherst, the hometown of Emily Dickinson, who wrote on whatever came to hand. If she had no paper, she would write on the back of a chocolate wrapper or an envelope. For her, the act of writing was as imperative as it was incendiary.

When I try to organize – my little Force explodes – and leaves me bare and charred.[5]

The act of writing is generally thought to be an explosion followed by organisation. Dickinson is suggesting that it is the attempt at organisation that brings about the explosion. A sampler she sewed as a child reflects this. With each line, she runs out of room and has to squeeze in words above and to the side. She neither measures the space nor unstitches and corrects her work.[6]

Dickinson's observation is from a letter to her mentor, Thomas Wentworth Higginson, which might be why she refers to her force as *little* even though it has such a decimating effect. She knew it wasn't and devoted her life to it without reservation but, to invite his attention, she makes herself small. Their correspondence is painful to read as Dickinson can't decide how to behave and veers between colleague, pupil, rebel, mystic and flirt. At times she writes as if to herself, as if working towards a poem, and at others as if performing obeisance.

I think you called me 'Wayward'. Will you help me improve?[7]

Higginson did not think her poems strong enough to stand up to publication. For one thing he found them too loosely made. Her phrases are suspended between dashes, like fragments held mid-air. While she took the trouble to make up her poems into roughly sewn bundles, she left variants on the page beside words she hadn't quite decided upon. She was honouring their nature as exploded matter.

(Anything written down is a disappointment of sorts. Even though it's the first time you've put the thing into words, it's a repetition. You've experienced it already. Then there is the fact of words on a page – they look so ordinary.)

—

In my sixties London primary school, we sat on hinged benches at double desks with inkwells, and practised a bland roundhand

29

that I found hard to regulate or sustain. We were being taught to organise ourselves and teachers spent all day adjusting us: slowing our pace, telling us to speak up or be quiet, to straighten our ties or pull up our socks, to wait, to hurry, to stand up or sit down, to pray, to sing. They insisted that we wrote alike and only with the right hand. When my left-handed brother was forced to do this, he produced mirror-writing. I regularly found myself in trouble without understanding why but I had no desire to rebel. School was a place of books and so, to a certain extent, I felt at ease there. The playground was terrifying but there was a library. I found a way to be present and absent, as I had at home.

Before I knew what I wanted to write about, I had a strong idea of what my writing should look like. It would not be round. I made no conscious connection between roundness and femininity but it seems obvious that that was what I was resisting. Roundness was also conventional. I didn't want to write the way I'd been told – writing was too important for that. In school books you can see my writing change from page to page as I experiment with styles. I gripped my pen in my fist as if it were a spear, and was forced to correct this, which only made my writing worse. I wanted my own style and found it – as with poetry or clothes – by trying on other people's. I copied my mother's barely-there elegant italics, managing a page of lumpen angles before I gave up. My father's writing intrigued me. It was angular and evasive, swooping and then huddled, stylised and wary.

I was trying to present myself as decisive, spiky and discerning, not mimicking the male but borrowing its attributes so as to attain its authority. This isn't what I thought then. I wasn't yet listening to the sound of my voice or envisaging anyone

30

else scrutinising my words on a page. So why did it matter what they looked like? Perhaps because writing was already so important to me that I wanted it to look like it should be taken seriously.

Even so I wrote impatiently, not bothering to form a word before rushing on to the next. I wanted minimal contact with the page, as if the actual writing was just something to get out of the way. I wanted the idea and the finished thing but the act itself was, and is, exhausting. There is something about the intensity and the exposure of recording a thought that still alarms me. The more scrutinised I feel, the worse my writing gets. Writing so that even I can't read it has become an important part of the process. The more urgent the thought I want to jot down, the less legible it will be. Someone recently described my writing as looking like hieroglyphics, and it is partly drawn – disjointed, pictorial, still awkward, the words almost unsaid.

The act of writing has remained a form of stepping aside which, for all the thinking and planning and revising later, I can't remember.

7. The refusal of place

The landscape that has been most formative to me is one I don't remember looking at. When I was eleven, we moved from London to a village in Essex. I refused to see where I was, a refusal so adamant that I abruptly became short-sighted. I refused to admit this was happening and refused to wear the glasses I was eventually prescribed. I didn't realise that refusal was very much in the Essex spirit. The county has long been a haven for those who will not conform or who insist that there is a less obvious, more interesting or rewarding way to live: dissenters, reformists, zealots, entrepreneurs, inventors, evaders, outsiders, insiders, radicals, chancers, artists, idealists, fanatics.

In the seventies, Essex was blurring into the city while refusing to become a suburb. It was in some ways deep country and in others nondescript, a place people never left and somewhere to pass through. To my inexperienced and failing eyes, the shapes this landscape made were unclear. Back then I would have described it as featureless, perhaps because that was how I saw myself. Full of unformed feeling and energy that lacked application, I wanted to be in a place that met me with drama. This meant the city and if not the city then at least a steep hill, high cliff or ruined cathedral. Essex didn't offer such easy charms. At first, I was bewildered. Then I tried briefly to become part of the landscape before embracing refusal. I decided not to bother being charming either. I refused to be a girl or to be clever, and having been told I didn't fit in, I refused to do that too.

I was writing all the time, in a teenage way, about other worlds and inner lives, unaware of the extent to which I was taking in the here and now. Writing was part of my all-round protest against being where I was, and for the seven years that I lived in Essex, I looked past it to my inevitable return to the city. The only attention I paid to Essex was in terms of it being the place I wanted to leave. It took me years to grasp how formative and powerful this made it. Home wasn't the problem, I thought, only Essex. I didn't yet understand that the home you leave behind, the one you grew up in, travels ahead and is always there in some form to greet you.

The plainness of this landscape demands attention to detail. You look at a mudflat and think *So?* But you look some more. I used to walk with my father across the mudflats and salt marshes beyond Bradwell nuclear power station. We'd stop off at the seventh-century St Peter's Chapel, which had been cobbled together out of Roman building waste and looked more like a billet or a public convenience. That mud was one of my early subjects. It is vivid and featureless and gives off a particular stink: a mixture of fish, milk, eggs, salt, tar, petrol and vinegar. I'm nostalgic for it now.

The life that that mud contained – shuffling crabs, dull snails, lugworms, cockles and mussels – lacked distinction. I didn't know this was one of the country's last wildernesses, that the stubby green plants were glasswort and eelgrass, and those creatures a vital source of food for what I thought of as small brown birds: redshanks, turnstones, curlews, dunlins. The naming of things makes them so much clearer that it becomes an end in itself. I never carried a book or asked my father or listened to him if he explained. I didn't want to be there so why learn names?

My energy went into getting out of the village as much as I could because life, action and drama were all going on somewhere out there and I couldn't reach them. No one would give me a lift and the bus did not come. One winter's night, some friends and I were so bored that we set out for a party that we weren't even sure was happening. No one seemed to quite know the address but the challenge of trying to get there gave us something to do. We walked out of the house and set off in as straight a line as we could across fields that had just been ploughed and were now frozen. It was so dark that I couldn't see either my friends or the gouged mud beneath my feet. We kept falling but were so young and cold that we felt nothing and kept going only to fall again, carrying each other through by laughing and yelling and making it into a story even as it was happening. I don't remember the party and can't be sure that we ever arrived. What has remained is the thrill of how we took charge of the matter. We wanted to leave the village and we did so by the simple act of walking away. It was as exhilarating as breaking a spell.

The spell was real. At my school, a local comprehensive, there were girls who were so bright that they could have done anything but no one suggested further education or any future that would have meant moving away. Many left school at sixteen and got married soon after. Some badly needed to move away. I saw the good and the bad of what it meant to be deeply rooted in a small place. I envied the certainty of belonging as much as I feared it. Thirty years later, I was driving through the region late on a Saturday night. As I approached the centre of a small market town, I thought there'd been an accident. People were lying all over the road – young women strewn about the place as if struck down by a terrible curse. They had been binge-drinking to the point where they were far off in the dark. Another way of breaking the spell.

I was refusing Essex by reading American poetry when I came across Denise Levertov's 'A Map of the Western Part of the County of Essex in England'. Her 1930s Essex childhood was a place where

> . . . only a haze of thin trees
> stood between the red doubledecker buses and the boar-hunt.[8]

All I had been looking at was that haze of thin trees. I had no interest in what lay on the other side of them. The place where I lived was everyone's idea of an English village with its five pubs, three churches and a chapel, bowls club, morris dancing and summer fete. I was in the last year of the primary school to be taught two classes to a room in the old Victorian schoolhouse. To me, the village had the type of historical detail that was useful only for postcards. I refused to think that somewhere I found so cut-off and dull could mean more.

The village put its dilapidated ancient halls to unlikely use. An East London church mission turned the seventeenth-century manor into a halfway house for psychiatric patients and another house into a boys' home. I found friends in both institutions.

Now these places are hotels, spas, apartments and country clubs. The last time I went back I got lost as there was a new road cutting across the route I knew. This was so disorientating that even after I arrived in the village, I stopped at a crossroads and had no idea where I was. I didn't trust the signpost because in my day the village boys had regularly turned it round (one sitting on another's shoulders) as if adjusting a clock.

The refusal of place might seem like an insistence on a wider world but it also means you're not listening. There were people I saw every day who had fought in wars or survived concentration camps. My Hungarian maths teacher, whom I feared and adored, had a number tattooed on his wrist. The crazy recluse who lived down the road from the school and was said to have buried a piano in his garden turned out to be Henri Chopin, an eminent French sound poet who lived through hell and then spent the rest of his life in radical experiment. There were many other, quieter, histories that I walked straight past, such was my hurry to be gone.

Essex can be both raucous and genteel. The only reading I've given that had a dress code was in Frinton, an Edwardian resort on the Essex coast that didn't have a pub until the twenty-first century. The event was at the golf club and the tickets were printed with the words 'NO JEANS'. I read a detailed passage about a post-mortem to a largely geriatric crowd who were unfazed. *Quite the thing*, a dapper gent with two sticks murmured as he hauled himself past on the way out. Driving back, I came across a pink stretch limousine that had got stuck trying to navigate a mini-roundabout.

The Essex I'm describing is one I remember and invented.

It's also one I absorbed far more than I knew. It went in deeply because of my resistance to it – as well as its resistance to me. When I go back there, I wonder if this mutual refusal will end and something will open, perhaps in us both. It never does and I am always relieved.

8. Small talk

As we embarked on adolescence, we started to talk like grown-ups, becoming adept at chat and using the currency of illness, tea and weather. *Not bad, could be worse. They say it'll rain. We could do with a drop of rain. Another cup? Don't mind if I do.* Men either said little or made statements and offered explanations. They spoke with immediate authority about any subject they felt to be worthy of their attention. Women used smaller words and gathered authority as they circled, hovered and swooped. *It's not my place to say. I wouldn't say only she did say. I don't like to say. Someone should say. Do you think I should say?*

Often I missed what was being said because I was distracted by what else someone was revealing. It could be a deep secret or a passing mood but it would roar. Sometimes I felt myself become a mirror, reflecting back what I saw, and I was punished for it. Joseph Conrad found the London streets terrifying because of all the passing human contact: 'I see their personalities all leaping out at me like *tigers*!'[9] For me, social gatherings were crowded with tigers.

I was as alarmed by the changes in my body, when they finally arrived, as I was eager for them. I didn't know how to arrange myself in front of a mirror, let alone in conversation, and was mortified by my mother's frank discussion of periods and puberty. She had been sent to a Swiss finishing school and was then a reluctant debutante before rebelling and going to medical school, and her conversation was a mixture of elegance, self-effacement, muted brilliance and clinical fact. She made a point of introducing such subjects not only in front of my brothers but their friends (boys!). At school, periods were whispered or joked about – *She's on the rag*. Girls asked each other if they'd *started yet* with a bluff competitiveness that made everyone defensive. You could get out of a PE lesson by saying you had your period but it was also used to dismiss your anger or distress: *Time of the month, is it, love?* We were taught about periods as an aside in a class about reproduction. They were a waste product, an incidental event. No one said that menstruation could make you double up in pain and vomit or that premenstrual dysphoria could be akin to psychosis.

I started a Saturday job in the village hairdresser's, which had been squeezed into the ground floor of an old cottage. The reception was a spindly table edged with a flounced satin curtain. There was an appointment book with a leatherette cover and a solid custard-coloured telephone. The atmosphere was of dried flowers, crochet, poodles, lipstick, doilies, Crimplene and talc cut with ammonia from the perm lotion and the industrial-strength florals of the shampoo. The peeling rosebud wallpaper was damp with mildew and steam.

There was a manageress (her emphatic term for herself) and three hairdressers. Anna was small, unsmiling and compact in her gestures. She said as little to me as possible as I stood beside her passing perm rods and papers, often in the wrong order or the wrong way round. She worked fast and I never seemed to be ready. Anna didn't address me directly and when, once again, she had to return a customer to the sink because I hadn't rinsed her hair properly, she complained to the manageress as if I weren't there. That kind but exasperated woman would sack me a few weeks later. Becky was tall and narrow, with long fingers and pointed nails. Her hair was a shiny aubergine, her skin strongly tanned and her eyes and lips coated in sticky plum. She also took little notice of me. I didn't mind. I was delighted to be there and to be thought (briefly) worthy of being given a role. There was so much to learn that I didn't mind if nobody spoke to me. The third, and friendliest, hairdresser was Martin, whose hair was a perfect auburn pageboy. I wasn't curious about why Martin wore floral blouses but I was jealous of his hair. One day I arrived and the manageress announced that from that day Martin would be known as Melanie and that was that.

Now that I was starting to look like a grown-up, I was allowed to hear the conversations that had been paused when I entered the room as a child. I was sent to make tea, which meant squeezing into the tiny back room where a couple of the hairdressers might be having a cigarette break. They would talk about aching legs and *sore boobs* and *not wanting it* or *not getting it*, and *he's a bit of* and *she's right up herself* and *did you know* and *have you heard* but there was no shrieking or giggling. They were barely ten feet away from the customers and so exchanged gossip, confessions and outrage in concise phrases between puffs on their cigarettes. They averted their eyes and kept their faces impassive as if talking to themselves. My presence didn't stop them but it might have made them less direct. Would I understand? Might I tell?

My mother, who I thought spoke so freely, gave me some advice. *There are three things a hairdresser should never discuss*

– *sex, politics and religion.* There was small talk and there was serious talk and each had its time and place but, now that I was thinking about it, all talk seemed to come down to one of these three things.

At a time when the proximity of other people was my greatest difficulty, I was faced with washing the hair of strangers. The intimacy of this act doesn't occur to the customer who is just tipping back her head and closing her eyes. Most of the women who came to the salon were old (to a thirteen-year-old) and I was as squeamish about ageing bodies as I was about my own. In the seventies, many women over forty dressed like women over sixty. Most had tightly permed hair so processed that it didn't seem to be hair at all. They wore sensible but feminine skirt suits and dresses, and sometimes slacks. There were always headscarves, gloves and brooches, and wool or nylon stockings but never bare legs. Clothes were worn on seasonal rotation – tweeds in winter, pastels in spring, florals in summer – in fabrics ranging from antique to synthetic. Whether they lived on a farm or in a hall or a council house, they carried the authority of their maturity. I don't remember seeing an older woman in the village fold herself away, defer to children or hesitate to issue a corrective. Nor do I remember seeing them be frivolous or silly (except sometimes among men), or become excited, angry or distressed. Why would I? We barely occupied the same sphere. If they came to our house, they spoke to my mother.

Washing a woman's hair, I would look down onto the relaxed face of someone who had no sense of being scrutinised. They were often thickly made up and Anna had trained me to keep the nozzle close to the skin and cup my free hand around it to

41

ensure that water didn't disturb their powder and foundation. I would gather a woman's hair in my hands to draw it back into the sink. The oldest hair was like the most delicate of bird's nests, something dry and fine and made mostly of air. Those puffed and permed helmets dissolved when wet into babyish strands. The women's faces seemed to share the same fixed expression – one that would rebuff the world before it met them. Never surprised, always prepared, they expected trouble, were suspicious of feeling and not fool enough to be impressed. All this dissolved too as they relaxed and I saw something of their younger selves.

One day, an elderly woman came in who'd had throat surgery. She spoke in wet burps that sounded both comical and obscene. I was warned (or imagined?) that there was still an open hole in her throat, hidden in the folds of her neck, and tried not to look as she settled back and, smiling, closed her eyes. At first I couldn't stop thinking about that hole in her throat and what would happen if I let the water or the shampoo trickle down her face. For most women who came to the salon, this was a rare moment of peace, but this woman without a proper voice did not stop talking. The ugliness of the sound she made was so powerful that I listened as hard as I could. I was holding her head and stroking her hair, and believed I understood.

When I got home from my first day at the hairdresser's – full of new knowledge about touch and overhearing and growing old – I discovered that my first period had begun. Perhaps because my mother had been so open about menstruation, I refused to say anything and only let her know by leaving my bloodstained underwear in the laundry basket for her to find. She said nothing either except to suggest that I soak them in salt and cold water before putting them in the machine.

The small talk I listened to was women speaking about matters of life and death. They talked of their bodies and passing time, of survival and danger. They passed on vital skills and let each other know that they too had endured that poison or that blade. They held each other's heads and hands, and made each other beautiful. They passed out weapons and shared maps. They took apart engines and rebuilt towers. They cast spells and dealt curses. They operated and they healed. They issued warnings and formed circles and set other women aside. They put on a white glove and ran a finger along a ledge to test for dust. They held up their freshly washed sheets to the light just as they held up those of others which were stained with semen or blood.

This talk could hold someone in place or cast them out. It was mostly indirect, an observation tilted towards no one in particular. It was far more powerful than direct address. Delivered in the form of something caught in the air, it moved easily from one person to another; its nature was to be dispersed.

The hairdressers could also be kind and when they realised that I wanted to look like them, styled my hair as if coiffing a doll. For one day I had a perfect pageboy too, but the next morning my hair was lank. I didn't have the hairdressers' hot tongs and potions and sprays with which to restore it, let alone their casual alchemical expertise.

When I arrived in the village, my hair had been long and tangled. Girls who ironed their flicks and sprayed their fringes each morning laughed at my head of snakes and turned away. I made myself take on the shape of these girls. I didn't want to be them, just to look like them enough not to attract attention. I wanted to be anyone – as in no one. I found a small voice for myself too. My small voice can still hold my writing voice in its grip. I back away from a serious thought with a joke or qualify an assertion to the extent that the reader notices only my reservations. The words start to wink, giggle and blush. As a woman taught that it is her role to relieve others of silence, I might start to gabble. Even if I wrest myself free of the habits of smallness, I need to do more than take on those of the loudly spoken. A large voice is not necessarily a loud one. A clear voice is more than a performance of style.

—

Women make themselves small so as to be allowed to stay in the room. We make small talk which we also use to ensure that we can safely pass by and go about the day. This is the soothing or smoothing of the world around us, a habit learnt early and profoundly ingrained. My mother went on long walks alone, which made me worry. *Aren't you afraid of walking alone in the woods? No. What if you met a man? I believe I would know what to say.*

A friend and I were sitting by a lit window on a summer's night. We hadn't shut the curtains. This was in the semi-derelict house that I was living in in the early eighties, one of six that hadn't been demolished. Opposite and round the corner there

44

was only wasteland and splayed metal fences. There seemed to be no one out there. I was twenty-one and often woke up alone in this crumbling building with a worn-out slippable lock on the front door. It was as if it wasn't a proper house, let alone a home, and the door was not a proper door. Once or twice men knocked and said they were *from the council* and needed to check our heating or wiring or roof. They would glance around, realise there was nothing worth stealing, and leave.

That night, there was a knock on the door and two men stepped inside as I opened it. *We saw you girls and thought we could come in and have some fun.* I kept my hand on the door. *The boys wouldn't like that*, I said. They laughed as if they knew there were no boys. *Where are the boys?* They took a step towards me but I did not step back. *They've gone to get some beer and will be back in a minute.* This they chose to believe. I shut the door and we laughed too because the situation was both terrifying and routine.

Like most women, I had such encounters from an early age. A man would, so to speak, step inside a door that I had not intended to open. I learnt to offer them a reason to step back again (other boys!) as if this was something they couldn't do for themselves. It was my responsibility to find the words that would enable a man who might be about to assault me to change his mind without losing face.

The first time, I said I needed to get back to my family. *Where are your family? Just through those trees.* The second time, I was on holiday and walking along the top of a wall when a man in the next garden came over for a chat. He then rubbed himself against me as if I were part of the wall. The incursion was swift and focused and he gripped my hips and held my eyes through-out. The words I might have said, the noise I should have made, had no time to take shape. Nor did I tell anyone. I was learning that I could be speechless to the extent that the words would take twenty years to form. The need not to say anything about what had happened ran more strongly in my blood than the need to protect myself. I somehow knew that to tell would be an *upset* – nothing would be able to remain in place and what I needed most right then was to step back out of that horrible dimension into a life where nothing had changed. I knew that here was something I had to keep rather than share because it could hurt others. It would spoil the holiday, embarrass my parents and their friends, who were friends of this man's.

There were other times when my body was handled in ways that made me abandon it. I left the room. Or did I? When I bring such occasions to mind, I look for myself and I am there only I've retreated inside myself. I cannot see or move or make a sound because my voice, my eyes, hands and feet are too far away. And I knew that these were things that *happened all the time* and were not so serious *in the greater scheme of things*. I heard the stories and watched the news. I wasn't bleeding or cut up or dead.

How do we know not to say? However open those around us might be, sometimes we still don't speak up. There were words for what happened but they would open doors that could not be closed again. If I could keep it small, something that happened between me and this man, then I had a place to put it and it might stay there and not bother me again. I did not want to find the words. I would not look for them.

9. The dark path

I transformed myself so as to be accepted by the disco girls at school. I changed what I could, which was how I spoke, dressed and behaved. These were not superficial changes. I was, briefly, that person through and through. We were all that person. Looking alike and doing everything en masse was a form of camouflage. What were we so urgently trying to hide? Maybe that we were coming into our power. Our deepest selves were demanding to be met.

This was a time of high feeling when anger sprang cleanly from the body in its electrical form. We were bewildered by our gathering potency and the blunt attention of not only boys but men, which was what we both feared and dreamt of. There were some who were at ease with this because their bodies changed quietly and conformed. They understood their power in its immediate sexual form and felt able to wield it. Those who approached them could be drawn in or held at a distance as they wished.

Some girls set themselves apart from the process. They grew quieter or younger. Or they starved, inflated or mutilated themselves – enactments we had no words for then. Some set out to swerve this phase entirely and became their mothers overnight. There were those who abandoned their bodies so successfully that they were taken aside and told to wash, and sometimes that they needed medical attention. We arrived in these categories and found it impossible to escape them, although there were those who did not find their place. The boy–girl dance was so dominant, so assumed, that it left little room for anyone to whom it did not make sense.

Sometimes the power that felt so unwelcome became a weapon in your hand. Even the most withdrawn and uncomfortable of us had felt this. We didn't yet understand that sex was only one of its aspects. How could we? The commentary we received from others was only about that. We rehearsed its effects and found people – often bewildered – on whom to practise. I wrote a declaration of love to a boy I barely knew but had fixed on as a subject. The letter was two pages long, and I can remember copying it out in a carefully feminine hand and lavishing attention on each phrase. Once it was posted, I didn't think about it, or the boy, again.

I was becoming aware that there was a dark path to follow inside myself and that it led back to my deepest imperatives. Everything came from this place – desire, pain, fear, curiosity, hope, determination – but I had difficulty telling one from the other. I lurched about, propelled by vast feelings that I didn't understand and exhausted by the scale of my responses.

And then I was fifteen and the strange silence fell. A year later, I started to panic. Perhaps I was shouting at myself to wake up. My body announced that it could operate without me and this changed my relationship with it for ever. Panic would always now be imminent. For years I planned every journey, even to the corner shop, on the basis of *what if.* The spontaneous socialising of my friends, open-ended nights spent drifting between pubs and clubs and parties, was too much of a challenge for someone who needed to know at every minute how they could get home. I carried maps and timetables, and prepared my exit. I stopped using the Underground and there were few buses at night. So I withdrew. I was thoughtless, heartless and irresponsible because I struggled to stay present, let alone in contact. Most of my energy went into simply feeling alright. I was so absorbed by my difficulties that I didn't realise my friends had grown used to my absence. I didn't turn up because sometimes I couldn't move. I wasn't there when they needed my help and so how could I ask for theirs?

The place I went to when I could not speak was also where my voice came from. The dark path established a way of going there and of coming back. I could turn things over and begin to understand their true qualities. What felt like becoming so small that I lost substance, presence and volition was actually a process of concentration. I went there to protect myself but also to form.

When people ask where poems come from, I can only say that I know when something might become one. I have a feeling of prickling alertness, somewhere between pleasure and a sense of threat. There is a presence I can't yet explain or make safe but which is recognised by my body at an animal level. I'm in the dark, as is the thing I've encountered, but there is a path and the lights are going on.

II

10. Amplification

In the midst of the disco girls, I'd been able to try out my voice without being heard. I sang and shrieked as loudly as I could but only when others did and in ways that were expected. My wish to fit in, to look and sound like everyone else, had come true to the extent that I didn't recognise myself. I wasn't speaking another language so much as making a borrowed noise. Soon I was making a different noise and it was equally borrowed: serious, ironic and smart. There was also the womanly noise I learnt to make when trying to smooth things over (moving my hands as I spoke as if perfecting a tablecloth). And there was a new noise gathering in what I was trying to write. It was no longer enough that my writing resolved a private tension. I wanted it to grow louder and move past me.

The first time I sang into a mic, I could barely hear myself. I wasn't even sure that what I did hear was me. A boy at school was having some friends round *for a jam* and asked three of us to come along to sing backing vocals. We were pleased because it meant being invited into male terrain even if it was just to enhance it. We arrived at the house on a winter's afternoon to find not only instruments but equipment. Arranged among coffee tables and armchairs were cables, amps and mics. We stood around in the chill air and the growing dim of the room. No one would have suggested turning the heating on (that was the dominion of parents) and no one hit a light switch. We were desperate for atmosphere.

It felt absurd to sing while huddled behind a sofa in someone else's house in the middle of the afternoon. But we sang what we were told to, when we were cued, slowly gathering confidence and volume. Even then it seemed as if someone had taken my voice away. Then I glimpsed it – or was it someone else's? – an *oo* or a *yeah* that managed to fight off the bass, guitar, drums and keyboard. There was no great explosion of noise. Either the equipment was timid or the boy was worried about his parents telling us to turn it down. He was singing the lead vocal but I could barely hear him either.

The three of us behind the other mic were bashful because we had, in general, stopped making noise. We strove to move slowly, speak quietly and behave like women. The feelings that we had applied more or less at random were becoming deeper and more intent. We were also beginning to listen to ourselves as our bodies continued to lead us through revised versions. We were young men and women now, not boys and girls, and we believed that we were equal and free. There had been marches, hunger strikes, protests and campaigns, and feminism had won. How could it not? I was too young to have been part of all that but I'd read the books even though I found other books more interesting, especially novels about difficult women and weary men.

We were not going to become our parents, some of whom said that they agreed with the idea of equality even as our homes were run, and our families structured, along traditional lines. Our relationships would be *modern*, which meant noncommittal and undefined. For a short while it seemed that we could have sex without risk from pregnancy or disease. It was easy to get a prescription for the contraceptive pill, which, like cigarettes and alcohol, was offered without warning. Syphilis was a scene in Ibsen or a story by Maupassant. We had not yet heard of herpes or HIV. No one asked permission and we did not know that it was ours to refuse. As for pornography, there were pictures and rumours, none of which seemed real. It was bad theatre that we did not seek to re-enact.

Why did I think the work had been done for me? That there was nothing more to do? We found that the dance was quickly set and it was the dance our parents had been doing all along. I went to parties and made a womanly noise just like my friends. We women – so grown-up! – positioned ourselves by the side of men in the form of neat and lovely shadows. Some hours into a party, those who were not watching or dancing or offering their bodies would gather in the kitchen to speak. At the end of the evening, which was sometimes the next morning, they would sweep floors and do the washing-up while the men slept. When the men woke, we made them tea. We were sixteen or seventeen and falling into place because, for all the books we read, what we lived was women drinking from small glasses and waiting to be asked and our mothers, despite their courage and genius and wit, silencing themselves.

Although I swept up glass and made tea after parties, I wasn't very good at being a shadow. I either didn't pay attention (although silent, the women were always attentive) or, if a conversation interested me, I would try to join in and not on backing vocals. I was either talkative or speechless and came away from conversation berating myself for one or the other. If I'd been chatty, anecdotal or opinionated, if I'd enjoyed myself, I would wake in the night burning with the shame of having commanded attention. I got excited by the unexpected connections that a conversation might make and felt compelled to announce them in the hope that between us, we could find more.

I worried about being too loud but I was always relieved when the music was turned right up so that we couldn't go on talking, or even listening, and just had to submit. I wanted music to overwhelm me and carry off the feelings I was finding it so difficult to have.

Much of life was observed or overheard. Parents might stipulate that a friend of the opposite sex was not allowed in your bedroom. There was no guaranteed way to talk to someone privately on the phone, no secret channel. At sixteen, if I wanted to make such a call, I left the house. I walked through the village, past three pubs and out beyond the first farm to where a phone box stood on a grass verge. There was plenty that could go wrong. Someone might be there already, in which case I had to wait— at first politely, invisibly in the dark, and then, if they took more than a minute or two, encroaching on the phone box's puddle of light. A grown-up would have rapped on the glass whereas I could not bring myself to reveal my impatience. Waiting was agony but all I could do was will them to finish. Did they not know that this was a matter of life and death? That I had to speak to him now?

Maybe no one was in (and nobody had an answering machine). I might get a wrong number or a crossed line and use up my money interrupting strangers. Or I'd get through and feed in the first of my stack of two-pence pieces only for it to be ignored or spat out, either way leaving me cut off. I had to ring the operator and persuade her to allow me two-pence-worth of time, about three minutes. Sometimes it all worked. I made the call, the boy was there and wanted to speak to me and, all of a sudden, I could hear him. He was intensely present – imagined and actual in the same moment. Our conversations were inept and brief, not least because calls were expensive. You used up your money and you did not ask people to ring you back. Calls were something in which you invested.

For those minutes that I could hear the voice of the boy I was in love with, or the silence between us, I listened hard. Then I walked slowly back, amplifying every syllable, stress, pause and intonation until the conversation became fixed as a song.

—

Waiting to hear a song was like waiting for a bus to arrive in that village. I would stand on the side of the road an hour after the bus was due, unable to accept that it wasn't about to turn up, sure that as soon as I got home and closed the door, it would. While waiting to hear what I liked on the radio, I had to listen to hours of other music, but then something else might catch my attention. I'd be excited about one song only to find myself distracted by another. Songs found me and made sure I kept coming across them until one day they were in my head and I wanted to hear them. I missed something I had not possessed. What more delicate form of seduction can there be?

I wanted a song to contain any number of recognisable things but to sound like nothing else. If it was going to stay interesting, it needed something running through it that would keep its sweetness shaken. Even the songs I loved most could settle and stop working. This might take weeks or years but when the end came, it was conclusive. If I met that song again, I'd be attentive but I wouldn't get drawn in. If I stopped listening before this happened, while a song was still doing something to me that I couldn't explain, then it might yet claim me.

If I wanted someone else to listen, I would leap up and down, wrenching the stylus away from one track and onto another. *Do you like this? You'll love this. What do you think? Great, isn't it? Isn't it?* At such moments, I wasn't listening, I was showing a song to someone. Once they'd got the gist of it, I wanted to show them another and another as if I could direct their curiosity as well as their listening. It was as if I'd given them a poem to read and sat beside them pointing at a phrase or a line break before they'd even got there. *Do you get it? Do you see?*

There are songs about pain that you can't help but dance to. If you hit the floor then you are alive to possibility rather than caught up in actuality. Forget the miserable words and be glad that you're still capable of being, in the broadest sense, seduced. And the song is there to reassure you that it's perfectly natural to be joyful and heartbroken at the same time. You can be crazy about one person while dancing with another because in music (as in poems) everything is both immediate and displaced.

Perhaps dancing is the ultimate form of amplification. You listen to a song and your body makes it louder. You become louder too – both more yourself and freed. I've always found dancing hard to resist and am ashamed of how much I want to do it. Sometimes I dance because I am feeling too shy to make conversation. Or I become overexcited – feeling! – and instantly try to contain this. Is a good song all it takes for me to abandon my measured self? Who is this alarming creature who feels compelled to throw herself around? I hold her back and try to dance as casually as those who are jigging on the spot while they chat. She unsettles me but I am in the end glad that I can be her: someone with an unseemly capacity for joy.

—

Soon after I started college, a group of boys who'd only just met revealed to each other that they were musicians. They turned to me, the nearest girl, and asked if I wanted to sing. I tried hard to sound indifferent but knew that I wanted to do this and that I was ashamed of this desire to make music with others, to join in. I arrived at the basement where we were going to play so nervous that I quickly drank whatever was offered to me so that I was quite drunk when we began. This time, the equipment was better and I heard a strong clear sound that turned out to be me. I started to form a relationship with the sound I was making and couldn't stop. It seemed incredibly firm and loud and took up the entire room. I forgot about the others and ignored their cues and went on singing more or less to myself. It was indicated to me afterwards that this *wasn't cool* and I blushed but didn't really care. I wasn't interested in what they were doing or even in how I sounded. I was fascinated by this new form of separation. I could hear myself.

This taught me that I needed to amplify what I wrote, to make it not louder but clearer. I needed to hear what it was trying to say. It isn't possible to listen to myself without creating this distance. It's a test, too, of how the words might reach someone who is just passing by.

—

When you write, who's listening? Some people go about it as if no one will read a word they say, not even themselves – it's getting the words down that counts. Others write as if they're constructing something for their own pleasure, a ship in a bottle that's locked in a box no one else will be able to open. There are also those who write as if everyone they know is standing at their shoulder (or another writer, or their mother or father). Others write in order to bring such a presence about. There are days when I can write only because I believe no one is listening and I will never see those words again, and others when I need to build a ship in a box that no one will open. Or I might need to turn round and face everyone crowding in behind my chair.

Listening is informed by where you are in relation to what you're hearing. A whisper in your ear or a shout across the street might be equally tantalising. In both cases, you can't quite see who's speaking because they're too close or too far away. In routine speech, we fall into place. We stand at a distance from each other that is agreed upon and undiscussed. Each of us is quick to feel encroached on or held away. We arrange ourselves as parts of speech.

I could not have imagined a life without music in it but the time came when I stopped listening. This wasn't because music stopped working. I am still transported within a split second to any particular time. The danger doesn't lie in what music makes me remember but in being reminded of just how much I used to feel. Even if the memory that the music belongs to is a difficult one, I am restored to the intoxication of feeling something that strongly, of having been so alive. There are times when I do not have the strength to feel, I can't risk it, and so do not listen – to music, to others or to myself.

I listen differently these days. It has become harder. The years of turning up the volume and standing near the speakers and playing in the band led to me developing tinnitus when I was twenty-one. There is a continuous shrill noise in my head like that made by an old television or stereo with loose wiring. Over the years it has hardened and grown louder, leading to hyperacusis, so that background sounds can be uncomfortably loud. I hear too much. I have to leave parties, concerts and cinemas because a sound level that seems perfectly tolerable to others is causing me pain.

When I was young, I wanted the world around me and the books I read to amplify what I felt. I lived in a quiet world where music, conversation and events largely occurred indoors. There were closing times and nothing happened on Sundays. To disrupt this hush felt as if it had meaning and so I turned up the music just as I turned up the volume of the language I used in my poems. It was safe to do this because no one was listening. I felt loud anyway because of the unease in my body and the activity in my mind.

Music was a bodily experience. It still is but I play it more quietly now and am drawn to its more subtle effects. When I reread something I loved thirty years ago, I take pleasure in the quiet phrase and the important role that small words play in tuning what is being said.

I have forgotten what it's like to experience silence although I need 'silence' in order to write – no background music or white-noise machine or human proximity. All I know is loose wires growing steadily louder. I am always listening now.

11. Singing along

Like many people, I can sing along to dozens of songs. I know every verse, chorus, whoop and sha-la-la but cannot conjure them from silence. I need to re-enact the listening by which I first learnt them in order to bring them to mind. But singing along is not about listening and the exuberance I feel doesn't come from hearing the song. It's about travelling alongside it and meeting every detail, and the pleasure of being restored to something I once knew.

There are those who can stay quiet while they enjoy this and then there are those, like me, who can't contain themselves. Even if I just murmur a phrase or mouth the words in silence, I have to do something. Late one summer night, I got into a cab and the driver was playing *The Dark Side of the Moon*. We travelled along peaceful lanes, the sky still luminous in the small hours, the windows open to the soft blue air, and I started to sing along. I kept my voice so quiet that it almost wasn't there, ashamed of this compulsion but willing to indulge it all the same. I listened to that album for about six months when I was an adolescent and have played it less than a dozen times since. I know all the words, notes, monologues and sound effects, and in that cab I couldn't contain this knowledge. The driver probably knew it equally well but did not choose to show this. It was his choice to listen to it, not mine, and his experience that I'd intruded upon.

Singing along is different to singing. I'm not doing it to be heard and am more likely to do it when alone, although it is still a performance. I'm showing myself, and sometimes others, that I once knew this song. There is a residue of the competitiveness of the record shop – *Of course I know this!* – but it's only myself I'm competing with. If someone else is around, I do all I can to stay quiet or adopt a comic edge in case anyone thinks I'm claiming I can sing like, in this case, Clare Torry. She was paid a flat fee of £30 (double the usual because it was a Sunday) for her defining, wordless vocal on *Dark Side of the Moon*'s 'The Great Gig in the Sky' – as if she herself were only singing along – and thirty years later won a court case for recognition and royalties.

As soon as I discovered music, I started to sing along. It was a natural extension of getting to know the song as in reading a poem aloud and so adding your voice to its own. It didn't occur to me that I was spoiling things for other people. My brother would punch me if I didn't shut up during *Top of the Pops* but I found it impossible to sit there and not react. A fight would break out, and my mother would march in and unplug the television. When I sing along now, I immediately worry that I'm being annoying (will someone march in and pull the plug?) and that I'm showing off, but I still don't entirely stop myself.

When others join in, singing along is a straightforward pleasure. No one's listening and everyone is allowing the music to release them into memory and feeling. We are not taking it seriously although, at the same time, we are indicating that for us music is a very serious matter indeed.

When I stood around in the record shop wanting to talk, when music was the most important thing in my life, I stopped singing along. There was so much not being said and that I was unable to express that I became speechless. I still learnt all the words but for now I just wanted to listen. Music was becoming a more interior pleasure and for all the competing in the shop over who had the best taste and the most information, I cared less and less what other people thought was good. This was happening in my reading too.

—

I don't have any of the poems or stories I wrote as a young child and don't remember thinking of them as either precious or private. But when I started to write about actual people, situations and feelings, I felt invested and potentially exposed. Just as I concealed myself behind a series of styles (tomboy, disco, hippy, punk), pulling one layer over another, I started to do something like that with my poems. It was inevitable that as I read more poetry I would have a stronger, but not a clearer, idea of what I wanted my own poems to sound like. Perhaps the aim was to sound so much like someone else that people forgot this was me. When I'd wanted to make noise, I had hidden among the disco girls, and now I was hiding my writing by replicating the noise made by what I read.

The first person I showed these 'grown-up' poems to was my friend Sophie, who recently returned a dozen of the letters I wrote to her between the ages of seventeen and twenty-two. I had added a few pages of my writing to one of these, making it sound like an afterthought and being careful not to declare any ambitions. This wasn't poetry, it was just *stuff*.

> I'm sending you some of the stuff I've written. Don't worry,
> not for an opinion, just because I want to.

That's pretty much what I would say if sending my poems to someone now. I'd be offhand so as to pre-empt any sense of obligation and would always give them an out. I don't remember Sophie's response and I wouldn't have minded if she didn't give one. The point was to experience what it felt like to send poems out into the world, to be read without me there to direct or explain.

I sent Sophie three pages, written in capitals with minimal punctuation. These are slabs of words that have been simultaneously over- and under-worked but then so had my feelings. I hadn't had time to find my voice, let alone listen to myself and work out what I wanted to say. The first is from when I was seventeen.

> Feeling dumb-tongued I often remember you my faithless
> friend and god you ripped deep spitting scorn with such
> cheap tenderness

The boy wasn't scornful or faithless and he found it easier to be tender than I did. I remained in love with him for years (something I eventually faced in another of my letters to Sophie). He was an excuse for writing a poem that was an imitation of a poem. My feelings weren't singing so much as singing along.

> Me in some crazy lighthouse
> hearing a couple of virgin ghosts

swinging around that deadly town from
'Why don't you love me' to 'That's assuming I don't love you.'

There's Bob Dylan in the first line, James Joyce in the second and Tom Waits in the third. The fourth is an actual conversation. Just as I cut out photos and slogans from the music press to paste on my wall, I was cutting and pasting what I listened to and read.

Books were not yet something I took for granted and I was slow to get used to making marks on their pages. In my student copy of Eliot's poems, I was making tentative conversation:

Portrait of a Lady   *recurrent topic of failure to connect*
You will see me any morning in the park
Reading the comics and the sporting page.   *release from artifice*
. . .
Are these ideas right or wrong?[1]   *undecided*

Even this is an imitation. I'm trying out the authoritative tone of my teachers and the critics I was starting to read, as if tone itself could make my thinking clearer. Perhaps it can when you're first trying to find a way to talk about what you think.

I was drawn to poets for one reason, only to be influenced by them for another. Sylvia Plath's drama led me to her technique. I read T. S. Eliot for his intensity but was most interested in his chronic sense of embarrassment. I thought I was reading John Donne and Elizabeth Bishop for their precision when what drew me was the thing I was most wary of in myself: excitement. I latched on to M. W. Croll's phrase 'not a thought, but a mind thinking', a description of baroque prose style that Bishop quotes in a letter. I was attracted to this notion of poetry as live action and didn't worry too much about how to make it live. The Croll quotation doesn't end there.

Not a thought, but a mind thinking . . . an idea separated from the act of experiencing it is not the idea that was experienced. The ardor of its conception in the mind is a necessary part of its truth.[2]

I was full of ideas but separated them right away from the moment of experiencing them. It was as if they had to be made safe. I didn't understand the importance of my excitement and that that was where the life of the idea lay. I thought that writing, like speaking, was an act of moderation (which it is) and hadn't yet grasped that the point was to make your excitement clear and that this was how to locate meaning and how to connect. It was safer and easier to focus on style but in imitating the under-excited bookish boy, I was limiting my voice.

It took years for me to begin to understand how much I wrote in imitation and that this was alright. It's a way of clearing a path, especially a dark one. All writing is to some extent imitation, even of yourself. I can still find myself singing along and need to keep writing until I break out of the song. The re-enactment of what's known is a form of self-encouragement. You don't notice the day that your voice becomes your own.

12. I stirred in my sleep

I left home in an uncertain way – crushed by poor exam results and troubled by a confusing love. A few months later, my father left too. The blanks intensified. While part of me was making quick, sure judgements about everything, I ignored it. Having deflected the attempts of one or two teachers to help when I sabotaged exams and disappeared from classes, I now wanted to be rescued. Only I didn't know how to ask for help or, when it was offered, how to receive it but if someone provided instruction or direction, I put my faith in them. Such was my uncertainty that I would base an important decision on a stranger's passing remark, as if others knew better simply by virtue of not being me.

Someone approached me at college. He had a sweet face and wore a belted raincoat that was a little too short and tight to be cool. He said he was putting a band together and he thought I looked like a singer. I received this suggestion as I did most others – not with yes or no so much as *Oh alright*. If he thought I could be a singer then I thought so too. The boy wasn't himself going to be in this band. He was our manager. I had no idea what a manager did. The first step, he said, was for me to do a demo. We agreed on an Alternative TV track, 'Facing Up to the Facts'.

He took me to a studio. I remember how small the booth was, the cream-and-beige plastic, and the shock of headphones. I couldn't see anyone else, I was doubly enclosed, and I was listening to myself. He was serious and I believed that I was too. I read books, had ideas and thought about stuff. I was confident that I knew how to inhabit the song. I had kissed people at stations. I had wanted and parted and faced up to the facts. But I wasn't serious about myself. That day, as he made me sing the song again and again, I stirred in my sleep and started to sing with a new level of attention. I focused on the phrasing. The song was harder than I'd thought. The melody barely moved. I sang its six lines over and over, pulling my voice into shape.

Sophie and I were living in different cities and we corresponded because we didn't have phones or couldn't afford calls. Reading my letters to her now, I find them both spontaneous and staged. I'm full of bravado, eye-rolls and exclamations, and laboriously ironic about romance, exams, illness, music and home. It's the voice of a certain type of youth in the early eighties, one who was nervous, elaborate and bookish as well as ostentatiously unambitious. I was working hard to appear offhand while caring far too much about the impression I was making.

The letters document the years in which Sophie lost both her parents, the love of her life had to go away and she returned home to raise her little sister. We were learning about death, disappearance, money and work, and that life really does have its fixed points. I was negotiating illness and family breakdown, complaining about exams while enthusing about books, trying to recover an ability to learn, starting to write and to sing and then stopping again.

9th March 1982

In all the chaos I've only just realised that I haven't told you where I've moved to. The lecherous landlord decided to try to make us pay the bills he'd said were included and then put an electricity meter in that ate up about £2 a day.

. . . we're going to record some tracks at the local studio soon and do some gigs (maan) at the end of April. Don't know about it all really . . . If there were any substance and solidity to our band I'd love to persuade H to write something about us.

I really wanted to become so independent and unperturbed but much as I hate to admit it I think I'm a little very attached to this one. In love? Put it this way, he doesn't irritate me.

I was nineteen, frightened and superstitious, proud that we were going to perform but needing to make a joke of it. I sound doubtful about the band's future while already imagining being written about. I'm mad about a boy but taking a stance. It's all so open, so clumsy.

Not mentioning the band begins in ordinary embarrassment. I wrote most of the lyrics and they are terrible. I was still caught in the first heat of poetry and intensified every phrase. It was difficult to find the right words so I used the ones that did the most work. I piled them up. Looking at my lyrics now, they seem to be about two things: heartbreak and freedom. Perhaps I wrote about heartbreak because that's what I'd grown up hearing women sing about and also because I was still in my teens and it was the safest form of feeling to allow. But something else runs through my words which speaks to everything

I've written about since – interruption, precariousness, incipience. I think of this now as matter I'm trying to grasp but my starting point, in these lyrics, is the opposite. I'm asserting a need for things to be out of place. This was written in the back of a poetry book during a seminar:

> All it needed was a flicker of what might have been a hand
> caught halfway with luminous intention
> the glimpse of a figure turning away in a corner
> a loose uncertainty would have kept me

It's not a song but I forced it to be one. I was always astonished that the other two in the band could take a dense piece of writing like this and find it a tune. My words still outweighed my voice, which is that of someone who doesn't believe she should be singing. I don't commit. There are times when I make a bit of a joke of it, posturing and swerving in case anyone thinks I expect to be taken seriously. It didn't occur to me to practise, to strengthen my voice or to treat it as an instrument. I felt unable to say that I couldn't sing in a particular key. My silence lay deeper than a fear of conflict, although it is true that I was afraid of making the person who'd paid the advance or who processed my voice angry. (How I wanted to belong!) I didn't expect to be told that I was good at anything, only that I was alright. *You're alright.* I wore bizarre outfits and made borrowed statements as if I could gather substance from the outside in. We were as sincere, clueless and hapless as most would-be bands. There are funny stories and I can laugh as I tell them. So what made it all so painful or dangerous to write about? Why

72

did I feel quite such shame, so many years later, that I withheld what should have been the culmination of the story? Was I, at forty, speechless? Am I still speechless now?

The other two members of the band were men a couple of years older than me. We hadn't known each other beforehand and so our relationship was based on music. Like my later friendships with other writers, our bond had a particular nature. It was part friend, part family and part lover but unlike any of the three. They were thoughtful and respectful and we remain friends, but in the band we were emphatically democratic, which didn't work at all. Usually, I agreed with their suggestions because it seemed to me that they did most of the work. They knew more or cared more, and so I went along with what they proposed: the name of the band, the arrangements, the cover of the album and the single we released. It wasn't as if I had any better ideas.

The shame is not that the band didn't last. The whole thing was so incidental that when it ended I felt only the pain of not belonging any more, of no longer being part of a group. I'm ashamed of all the times I should have spoken up but didn't. That I took the wrong things seriously and others – like singing or my instincts, boundaries and judgement – not seriously enough. When our record contract was explained, and I was told I'd get half the royalties because I wrote the words, I made them adjust it. It didn't seem fair. My words were such a small part of it.

Men of my generation still sometimes test me on music. After ten or fifteen minutes of conversational interrogation, and with just the right level of surprise, they might offer a nod or even announce that I'm *alright*. At some level, I'm still relieved to have earned their approval. Back then it was mostly men who played the instruments, drafted the contracts, organised the venues, took the money, paid the money, mixed the sound, controlled the lighting, made the deal, wrote the review, played the record, and opened and closed the doors. They didn't object to me so much as lack curiosity, and treated me with an inert courtesy. Or they spoke to each other as if I weren't there, dropping into a more grown-up and invested conversation – the way I later saw male writers do too.

Our first gig was a support slot at the Beet Bop Club and, in the incidental manner of the times, it was reviewed in *Sounds*. The club took place in the London Music Co-op in Camden Town. The bare, cold room didn't surprise me, nor the fact that we had to get drinks from, and use the toilets of, the pub across the road. It was like a lot of other rooms where I went to hear bands, a bleak space run by men who appeared chronically un-impressed. I respected them as *proper* music people, although I took their hard work and history for granted. The audience were benevolent but took little notice. They weren't expecting us to be good, only interesting. We played as we might in our bedrooms, making no attempt to turn it into a performance. Somehow, the spare and wobbly thing we were doing worked. All that we'd built fell into place. We each knew where the other was going and met there. And I was absolutely *there*, fighting perpetual shapeless fear, having left the house to stand on a stage in front of a crowd and sing.

11th October 1982

. . . we're full of new material and have a gig with Durutti Column on Nov. 18th except D.C. may pull out due to illness but we'll still do it with someone else and then in December poss. support Section 25 again at University of London Union (where we saw Bauhaus) and a couple of other dates.

We've got a few good bands on here. Channel Four filmed Monochrome Set and The Passage. Also Eyeless in Gaza who are so good . . . [The boy manager] semi-manages them and Section 25 and does his own poetry readings (got an interview in *NME* last week). Trouble is he's better as a manager and organiser (really good) and will probably end up not performing at all.

I had stepped into the world of the bands I listened to but still felt like a child watching grown-ups attending to their work. Others moved around me and looked past me, going about their business, which was esoteric, expert and not mine. Three months later, I was squaring up to my finals and we were about to record. I couldn't even remember the name of the record company who I told Sophie were interested.

20th January 1983

People are asking me if I've got a job yet 'after all it's only six months to go' . . . I just look blank and wish I had the guts to say that I'm going to be a singer for a while and after that, go away for a while, etc. . . . Next week we are going to Luton to go to a studio and record 2 tracks that might become a single as some record company is interested. We are also doing a gig at the Haçienda in Manchester on Feb 3rd. Excuse my ignorance, but is that anywhere near you? [Lancaster] Could you possibly come?

We were going to sign to one label and then we signed to another. I remember the strangeness of arriving in a white-stucco part of London where people had offices. I don't think I'd been into an office before. The company was run by two men I thought of as a splenetic genie and a groovy dad. They were perpetually uninterested in what we were doing. It was like being sent to the headmaster only for him to wonder why you were there. When they gave us an advance, the genie stipulated that some of it was for me to go and buy *some decent clothes*. I bought exaggerated versions of the drab and peculiar outfits I already wore.

10th February 1983

Don't worry about missing the Haçienda. I wouldn't expect you to spend half a night in a station.

We went on at 10.45 by which time we were rather drunk. There were very few people there and I found the club quite disappointing after its reputation as a brilliant piece of interior design. It's full of girders and road signs but they're so shiny and new it's more like Legoland than bleak industrial. We enjoyed ourselves and got a good response from the 30 or 40 people. Then we got the 12.30 train home and ended up eating a burger and chips in King's Cross at 5.30 a.m. thinking 'This is the life of rock and roll!'

Do you have central heating? We have gas fires so when you get up and climb out of pyjamas, jumpers, socks, sleeping bag, quilt and blankets, you nearly die of frostbite. Then at college the library is so warm that I just fall asleep.

I wasn't connecting anything up – what was going on in my body with what was happening in my head, the worry about revision with the idea of doing some, not being a good singer with my lack of practice, the late nights and drinking. But I was sharing my words with other people now and the band was the first step with that as well. I remained far back in myself, receiving the news of what we were going to record and how it would sound. But when we were making the record, I sang all the time and my voice strengthened. I became used to hearing it and to discussing it with others. Being in a band became what I did. It gave me a solid place to be at a time when I needed one. It was also a sidestep away from the conflicting desires for romance and freedom that I was singing about.

10th May 1983

I, due to having a contract, am a professional singer! And we are recording a single (also available on twelve-inch) next weekend. The A-side is let's go commercial and do a cover version . . . After my finals, we're recording the album, no cover versions.

Last Saturday, after a day of recording the drum tracks for the album and single, we went to our first muso-biz party. Well, we almost did. Our record label were having a party in one of their protégé's houses, to celebrate the release of his album. We were very tired and got as far as the pub up the road from where it was all going to be happening. After an hour or two of business talk, we couldn't face the party so we went home. Was that cool?!

Two weeks before my finals began, we signed a contract. This was the only time I asserted myself. The genie said the contract was standard and that we shouldn't bother with the cost of getting a lawyer. I read it and insisted on some changes including the number of songs we would write each year.

Our music easily lost its way. We were given a producer who had a vision of the shiny sound he could turn our music into. The men got excited about the new technology in the studio and came up with multi-layered arrangements. It was like being in an acoustic hall of mirrors as the producer tried to bounce and double what we did into palatial pop. The record is four people undertaking separate experiments and has little to do with the music we made. We weren't clear or determined enough to survive this, and that was that. The record company never got the songs per year their contract demanded, nor did they want them.

The tapes we made of our bedroom rehearsals don't trouble me. However raw they sound, they sound like us. But I'm still reluctant to name the band because if anyone listens to the record, I want to be there beside them saying *We didn't really sound like that. Let me play you a cassette of one of our rehearsals instead. I didn't write the lyrics on that one. Don't you hate my voice? I hate my voice.* It's the voice of someone who doesn't know what she wants to sound like but who is also unhappy about what's being done to that sound.

Our single was released that September, on the day we supported a band whose lead singer had been my one friend in the Essex village. He would invent dance routines for us to perform to David Bowie tracks at the youth-club disco. We'd been close for years and then his time in the boys' home came to an end and he disappeared back into the city. Now he was in a band I'd seen on television. How could I behave like a singer in front of someone who knew who I really was? The great love of my teenage years also came along to the gig, bringing his own great love with him. The songs I sang were mostly about him but it didn't feel like that at all. On stage, all of that disappeared because I did too. I still get nervous before going on stage and feel exhausted afterwards, but if things go well I can achieve that moment of disappearance. The words carry because I'm no longer in their way and my body relaxes into a state of tremendous peace.

13. Hesitation

I'm trying to remember how the band came to an end. I had a vague feeling of being kicked out but apparently it became clear that I wanted to *go in a different direction.* I felt the same inertia that I had when asked to join: *Oh alright.* I knew by then I wasn't a good enough singer and also that I couldn't write songs. I didn't understand how to separate words from the music they already possessed and so had no idea how to construct a melody. The boy manager and the record-company genie were now telling me that I couldn't sing after all. The boy manager played me one of our tracks over and over, pointing out a single note he said I'd got wrong. He sent me back into the studio and I sang it again, exactly the same, only now you could hear it being dropped in. He had proved how carefully he listened and he'd let me know that I was a disappointment. I could only agree.

I graduated and wasn't well and all I wanted to do was go home, which I did for a couple of months. It was as if college and the band had never happened. Then I moved back to the city into the short-life housing co-op which gave me a room for £5 a week. My letters to Sophie record that I planned to emigrate to Canada or to become a teacher. I volunteered at a school for what were then called 'maladjusted children'. I thought I might go to an evening class to get a typing certificate and perhaps do a course in 'learning to use word processors'. I was fighting with the committee of the housing co-op as well as with the druggie who lived upstairs. I railed against coupledom and domesticity as I slid into both. I was still using a young person's irony to protect myself but I was also letting slip my hopes and dreams.

16th February 1984

Sending off CVs and phoning up agencies and trying to sound like a terribly jolly bright young thing with bags of confidence and oodles of enthusiasm. Yeah. I'm also being naive enough to write off to a few publishers and a couple of museums. I'd love to work in the V&A or the Tate but most of all the hallowed library of the British Museum.

3rd March 1984

My latest career choice is publishing as I have decided to get some practical and professional skills so that I can finally emigrate . . . But I'm still nagged by thoughts of wanting to work with young people with psychological problems or just to do something directly useful and helpful.

Being on the dole makes you realise that it is sickeningly true that in order to live freely and privately, and to be able to go where you want and do what you want, you've got to establish yourself as a Professional Person and doing so always involves shitty jobs and lots of crawling and lying . . .

. . . it seems as if nothing's changed for months. It has though, with a little sun now and again, a little less money every week, and what's most important I suppose, a renewed

interest in writing is lurking inside me and some of the ideas
I am having are actually making me want to try and get them
on paper.

I'd started my first proper job and was reading Doris Lessing and Alice Walker (both lent to me by Sophie), and having
thoughts about writing that I wanted to share. The job was as
a receptionist. The man I called the Cunt used to arrive at the
office shortly after me in the morning. He would take a shit
in the bathroom next to my desk even though he had his own
bathroom upstairs. I had to sit there in his stink, which the
people who then arrived assumed was mine.

7th April 1984

. . . the first person I met was the senior partner (the Cunt)
and he just said 'There's the switchboard, be polite and
helpful' . . . At first I was terrified but I soon learnt . . . the
only difficult things are remembering who's on Hold and
whether you need to Join or Withdraw or Cancel or all
three . . . I'm learning! . . . The most stressful time this week
was on Thursday when the Cunt wanted me to do some
photocopying for him. He then produced 15 thick files of
documents and said he wanted them returned in the exact
order they were, with all the bits attached to each other as
they were and so on. It took me 9 hours to do 750 documents
and then put all the copies in chronological order.
I started reading The Golden Notebook . . . I read the
preface on the train and bus and it was one of those pieces of
writing that make me feel really good because I feel christ this

is the way I feel about that, you know, just recognising your own seemingly incommunicable thoughts in an articulate piece of writing. I read more of it and then started simultaneously on The Color Purple. That one I really can't put down. The feelings behind it seem, like Doris Lessing, to cover so many different ideas that really shouldn't be separated but are usually separated or simplified because most people are incapable of describing them as a whole and making that whole comprehensible. It so often seems that there is a lot missing from a piece of writing, all the aspects of an idea that connect it to another idea . . .

I go on to praise Walker and Lessing for producing

a gripping piece of writing that touches so many different but intricately connected impulses inside you that if someone asks you what the book is about you can't say anything because you don't know where to start.

But you really know what that book is about, because you immediately recognise the feelings it evokes. I'll take care of these books and bring them back to you soon.

I was struggling to articulate the perfect experience of reading while at the same time trying to figure out how it worked.

I took Sophie's copy of *The Golden Notebook* with me to the launderette, which was run by a fierce, majestic Irishwoman who stalked up and down swigging Special Brew. She caught sight of the back cover, which said something about being a free woman. *So are you a free woman?* she demanded.

Are ya? Was I? My life was humdrum and uncertain. I was scribbling in notebooks, temping as a receptionist and living in what was virtually a squat. I had no real interest in making money or having a career. While I had no idea what direction I was about to take, I did feel driven. I just didn't know by what. It had something to do with writing and it was bound up with freedom.

The steps I took to undermine myself were a way of remaining free. I made sure I wasn't loud enough or clear enough. I didn't *sing up*. I was overcome by weariness in conversations, interviews and exams. I made myself strange, drove people away, and left home again and again, wherever and whoever it might be. These were useful points of hesitation. When I was unsure what to commit to (a book or home or job), they gave me a chance to revisit what I might need.

It's possible that, in the name of freedom, I will commit to nothing – I am after all *a free woman!* – but what then? I will be stuck where I am, among what I already know and within what I have already completed. Where's the freedom in that?

The question of how to live is not one I have solved and while I think about it most days, I hesitate to commit to an answer. I am uncomfortable about what that answer might cost.

14. What happened

As with my first notebook, I began to keep a diary because I was given one. I was sixteen and it seemed oddly grown-up, as if I'd been given a saucepan or gardening gloves. It was pocket-sized with a dull-green leatherette cover and had been made for the Town & Country Building Society. Perhaps my friend's father worked there. I had no idea what a building society was. It listed Useful Addresses and Telephone Numbers including departments for births, marriages, deaths and passports, tax offices and embassies. Each of these had a physical address and a direct number. There were also details of the Stock Exchange, wine vintages and pension schemes.

Although I've kept a diary for the subsequent forty years, I have never recorded anything much beyond events. From the start, I used a line or shape as a way of noting something without having to say it. In 1980, there's a day covered in triangles and I know exactly what that was about. There are abstract lines on most pages, cutting across days as a clear indication of a certain mood. The week of my eighteenth birthday is two loose spirals and the next four weeks of my last summer before leaving home are a flat continuous line. I'm doing nothing but waiting. In September, as I prepare to leave and have received my poor results, the line sags. When I look at these diagrams, the feeling of that time comes back to me. There's a series of zigzags on the day I was asked to come home because my father was leaving. I still don't have the words for that.

I don't know what happened in January 1979 because I've torn that month out. I'd tried to use the diary properly and write about what I felt but four weeks of that was enough. The opening entry is 2nd February – 'SID VICIOUS DIED OF A HEROIN OVERDOSE'. By 5th February, I'm writing half a dozen words at most. Now and then I try to be witty but mostly I can't be bothered.

I write in capital letters, perhaps as a way of appearing confident. I give as much importance to eating steak or going to the optician's as I do to having a date. On most pages I've tried to delete something, scoring it out so thoroughly that it's almost impossible to read. When I can make some of this out now, there's nothing to hide. I'm trying too hard to conceal my mistakes. I include the odd ironic overexcitement but mostly I list parties, bands, family occasions and essay titles (*'L'égalité entre les sexes crée la guerre des sexes – discutez'*). Now and then I go to an exhibition. In the back I'm adding up what I'm earning from my Saturday and holiday jobs, listing bus times, sketching maps. There are lists.

Dye
linen
plimsolls
John Ford
PVC

For 1980, I used a photographic-company diary. Its lists

86

were of gentlemen's clubs, airports, restaurants and hotels. It's a diary for a photographer about town, not a teenager who's still using capital letters. I fill in every personal detail required of me including blood group, passport number and bank numbers. I do this the next year and then cross it all out. By 1983, my writing is lower-case, often tiny and has settled into its strange spikiness. I'm listing essays and what I'm reading, hospital appointments and rehearsals, films and exhibitions but not many parties. I visit Sissinghurst and go to hear Joseph Beuys lecture at the V&A. The band is documented as

rehearsal
signed recording contract
studio
gig
photo session
test pressing
interview with Zigzag
~~Gig Upstairs at Ronnie Scott's~~

By 1984 I'm keeping up with my friends, their birthdays, my grandmother's birthday. My mother was insistent that I went to my graduation and I tried. The day's entry reads 'Mum 2 p.m. station, Dad – 6 foyer'. I was unwell and the day is crossed out. There is the time and place of my best friend's mother's funeral and next to it an appointment at the same time for a job interview. The day we move out of our family home I note only that my mother is starting her new job and what time the removal van is due. The circle code is back.

On almost every page there are sums, £12 and £8 and £4.50. The writing breaks down at the back, where I'm rehearsing an argument for a student grant: 'London now sometimes home sometimes London will return [the last word barely legible] home.' I've torn the next two pages out and the diary ends with a pathetically domestic list:

mirror
plant pots
shelves
recipes

There are phrases I'm trying out which would become poems or songs. They're scribbled down among the rest of life, in whatever space I have available. The lists continue:

phone
gas
elec
wiring
skip
van
insurance

wool
oil
heaters
cake

I insert reminders to pay rent but nothing about my periods until I'm twenty-two. The first entry for 1985, in capitals, is 'PERIOD' (on the same day that I give blood). There are sporadic codes which could mean anything from I had spoken to someone to I'd slept with someone or had a panic attack.

I give up the capital letters in 1988. As a new mother, I'm too tired. I start to write a poem in the back of my diary but thoroughly cross it out. There are sketched maps and directions: '100 yds along row of shops. Entrance to Peugeot garage. Turn R down back alley. 2nd one along.' In 1989, I make lists of poems: those to revise, those to finish and those to send out. Three of these made it into my first book.

In 1990, I invested in a more stylish diary with more space for my busier days. I abandoned it in June when I started a new job and bought a Filofax because my boss had one. There are a lot of notes on work and housing. I go to readings as much as I used to go to see bands. There's an interview at a nursery school for my daughter but no record of her father moving out. It was my decision, as hard as it was clear.

In 1993, I scribble a note about the archive of the planning of the reservoir near my village in Essex and the seed of a related story. 'Architect obsession with her because of her relation and similarity to someone else – or an extraordinary coincidence that is ultimately an obsession.' Eight years later this became my first novel.

15. Lyrical, domestic

> The men were dead, you see, and the women didn't marry
> so much because there was no one for them to marry and so
> they had leisure, and, I think, in a good many cases they had
> money because their brothers were dead, and all that would
> tend to writing, wouldn't it, being single, and having some
> money, and having the time – having no men, you see.
>
> Ivy Compton-Burnett[3]

The times in my life when I have loved without qualification and entirely unarmed myself, I've stopped being afraid of both life and death. I have felt at home. Motherhood has been the foremost of those times. I was pregnant at twenty-four and my daughter is so intrinsic to me that I've never thought to explain, justify or question her presence.

Writing is also intrinsic and unquestionable, although I've struggled to protect the conditions it requires. This has been a problem of time and money but also because I've lacked the conviction that writing is my work. At certain times I've had a room of my own and at others I haven't. Once, there was a room but I wasn't allowed to use it. It sat empty while I had to work within view. Still I turned inwards and slipped out of sight and was punished for it.

Living alongside another person has succeeded only when they have a different but equally compelling form of movement.

It might equally compelling be outwards rather than inwards but it has to be one that takes them away. Presence and absence reconcile themselves in my daughter. When I'm with her I am only her mother, but she is also the one person whose proximity never feels like a constraint.

My daughter's father was a kind man, modest and unenquiring. He would come to collect me when I was struck down by panic and never asked me to explain. We met when I joined the housing co-op and moved into the place he lived in. We had no heating or proper flooring but paid so little rent that we felt able not to have a plan. In the mid-eighties, London still had the give, the pockets and loopholes, that made this possible. I temped in offices and he worked as a dispatch rider, having dropped out of art school. His father had recently died and mine had disappeared into a new life. We came from large families and were close to our siblings. His were already having children of their own. He was also the manifestation of one of my childhood heroes. His grandfather wrote and illustrated children's books which featured a boy of his name with a shock of blond hair. I had loved the books and lived in their world, so when I met the boy with a shock of blond hair perhaps I felt a pull towards home. The books were about going to sea, and he and I were both at sea at this time.

Others came and went from the house including Sophie, who lived with us for a while. One night, she and I were so cold that we broke up a chair and burnt it. We could laugh about this because we were young and confident that life was still a matter of moving through and on. We didn't understand the privilege of that assumption or that soon we would move less easily and might become lost or trapped. Sophie was about to have to return home to bring up her little sister, and the home I'd been so eager to get away from was no longer there.

My desire to leave home had been gathering momentum all my life. From early childhood, I would just walk away, which was what my father did too. Now the only plan I'd ever made, to leave the country, inverted itself. I wanted a home. More than that, I wanted to return to a version of home that never existed, a place where I would feel at home, which was somewhere I've never been. My mother, having run the house and family for twenty-five years, moved to a flat and decided that she would keep no more possessions than she could fit into her car. I was proud of her for this but for the next few years I clung on to all kinds of junk just because I had grown up with it, as if I could import my lost home into any new one.

—

Whenever I publish a book, I feel profoundly sad. People suggest that this is some sort of post-partum depression and I want to kick them. I do not mother my work and a book is not a child from whom I am now being separated. I have come to realise that each book is a home.

My very first book was one I made myself, set in hot metal and hand-sewn. I followed up on a friend's passing suggestion – *Oh alright* – and spent a year at the London College of Printing because I wanted to work with books. The course was run by men who'd served a seven-year print apprenticeship and whose skills were being made obsolete by new technology. They were patient, generous and open-minded, and while they taught us how to use computers, we had to start with hot metal. We learnt about fonts by holding letters in our hands and then setting them in a stick which was then cast. Fitting letters together makes you think about their detail – the slab or hairline serif, the x-height, the kern, the ascenders and descenders. I was taught to pay attention to the shape a word makes on the page, its scale and substance in relation to the space, the line, the other words.

A couple of years later, I became editorial assistant to Margaret Busby, who had been Britain's youngest publisher as well as Britain's first black woman publisher. With characteristic rigour, she interviewed me twice – once in the office and once in the pub – while setting me a copy-editing test in between. Margaret taught me about publishing but also about what is possible if you decide to act. She went about things without fear or reservation: 'Our idea of distribution was stopping people on the street and asking them to buy our books.' I had made my own music and my own book but only because others had rendered it possible. I had not stopped anyone on the street.

Each morning, I rode on a feeble motorbike from crumbling rooms in South London to crumbling rooms in Soho. I had a typewriter, a telephone, an electric bar fire and a mug. My room was at the top of a dark staircase where fungi elaborated themselves in every corner. I watched tailors in the rooms opposite magicking up suits. I copy-edited manuscripts and corrected proofs, and discovered how much I enjoyed contemplating the rightness of a comma, a clash of adjectives or the use of a tense. Home and the world made a new connection. I was writing poems and now I worked for a firm that published them. I began to meet poets and eventually said out loud that I wrote poems too.

My diary for 1987 is as concise as any other. Over the preceding winter I note hospital appointments, the only record of a minor cancer scare that raised the possibility of losing my fertility. I have never been able to imagine the future and hadn't thought about whether or not I wanted children. I didn't think about where I'd be the next week, let alone by the time I was forty. That was the traditional age by which everything ought to be settled and my parents' generation were the first to disrupt this, mostly by getting divorced. The model I'd been given of family and home was now demolishing itself.

My daughter's father and I had moved four times in three years, from one rundown place to another. Despite how contingent and rudimentary our living arrangements were, I entered a domestic dream. I was planting, pickling, baking and knitting, arranging objects, painting the crumbling walls and rotting floorboards, and inviting friends round for meals, spending scarce money on elaborate ingredients. Our last move was into a flat which was more secure. We had solid floors and a gas fire, although one room was too damp to be habitable. I wrote 'TEST: POSITIVE' on 5th February. The next day:

2 oz crystallised fruit
maize flour
fresh pineapple
register with doctor

Someone had access to free theatre tickets and I went to see a lot of plays including Lorca's *House of Bernarda Alba*. I remember sitting in the dark and wondering what on earth I was doing as I watched a play about women who could not direct their own lives. It took a drama set in nineteenth-century Spain for me to begin to grasp the extent to which I'd redirected mine. The pregnancy was confirmed but unannounced, a new fact and an immediate secret. A week later I saw *Who's Afraid of Virginia Woolf?* It was as if I were exploring different versions of the domestic trap.

In May I planned to go to a parentcraft class but crossed it out. The publishing company was bought out and I lost my job and had to navigate a welfare system that expected people out of work to become entrepreneurs.

I was also writing a play about Galileo and planning to put it on with a friend. My mother carefully observed that I might be too busy.

Stanislavski
through line
super objective emotional memory
2nd wife
lipstick on edges of furniture
dog on wheels
daughter plays with an egg

In August there was a labour ward tour:

7 p.m. prompt
chairs on landing outside lift

Labour, delivery, pain relief
diet
layette
infant feeding
emotions and relationships

I didn't note anything that was actually said but I had more urgent concerns. 'Employment rights for the expectant mother (don't work over 8 weeks without MONEY).' At the back of my diary are notes I made as a freelance researcher on paddle steamers, ferries and nautical museums. Heavily pregnant, I was tramping around London from one library or archive to another, writing entries for visual dictionaries.

I wasn't sleeping much by then and realised that these small hours were some of the last I would spend as my old self, as in not a mother, who was someone I was about to become but hadn't met yet. I used to pace about reading poetry and mostly one long poem, Tony Harrison's *V*. I would walk back and forth, rocking the baby in my womb, intoning rhyming quatrains about cemeteries, graffiti, beer, bread, class, family, immigration, fascism, the miners' strike, education and death.

In October, Britain experienced its so-called hurricane. I listened all night as the wind hurtled around between blocks of flats. The sound was immense and abstract, as if the air itself were being ripped up. Then on 5th November: 'THE BABY DUE'. I was restless and wanting to walk so set off for the cemetery just as the sun was going down. I went there often, lingering to read the graves of children. Fallen trees had wrenched open Victorian graves and smashed sarcophagi. I wanted and didn't want to look. As the sun disappeared, I arrived at the tall spiked wrought-iron gates to find they were locked. There was nothing for it but to walk right across the cemetery to the other gate and hope to get out there. I carried my unborn baby through the dark and the dead and the fallen branches, and wasn't afraid because I was protecting her. I met my new self in this courage.

I was in labour for thirty-six hours and for much of that time could not bear to stay still. I walked the hospital corridors, naked under a half-done-up gown, tireless and oblivious. On the day she arrived, I wrote her full name, weight (in metric and imperial), length and head circumference in my diary. Five days later, in an exhausted scrawl, 'home'.

—

11th January 1988

I've spent one of my last maternity benefit cheques on a course at the poetry centre beginning next week. I handed over the money before I could change my mind.

Having a child made the imperative to write clearer. I discovered the Poetry Society, which was within walking distance. They were running a workshop (I'd never heard of a workshop) on a Wednesday night. My daughter was ten weeks old when it started and I figured I could make it there and back between feeds. The tutor was Fred D'Aguiar, and I learnt so much from him so quickly that one day I arrived with a draft I was proud of and, as it came off the photocopier and I caught sight of it again and again, I realised how bad it was and dropped it in the bin. When someone praised a poem of mine that was particularly florid, Fred said that it read like something written by a precocious eleven-year-old schoolboy. The group flinched but I knew what he meant. I had badly wanted to be one of those boys (at school, in the record shop, in the band) and I was still trying to impress them, still trying to get them to let me in. And so much of what I'd been taught as great literature was the work of clever boys. I had absorbed their nature.

Fred somehow showed me what to do without telling me. He was only two years older than me but in terms of his poetry a decade ahead. He had published his first collection at twenty-five, the age I was when I arrived in that room with my schoolboy poems. He'd already won prizes and he had found his voice. I realised that Fred thought I was strong enough to be told how bad those poems were and that I was ready to try harder. He gave me the confidence to expect more of what I produced.

When my daughter was eight weeks old, before I started the workshop, I had returned to freelance editing. Her father went back to college and so I was the main breadwinner. A few months later Margaret Busby gave me another job, at her new firm, and I was back among books. Editing taught me about the long process of arriving at a version that feels like the actual thing. Writing, and a writing voice, go through a series of arrests as they are evolved, corrected, adjusted and tuned. I was typing out my poems now and retyping them each time I changed so much as a single word or comma. I don't think I have ever known my work so well but I have no nostalgia for the process.

I had to get used to sending poems out into the world, and to accept that they would be met with *No* or *Not quite* more often than with *Yes*. I had thought of the literary world as a place of older men and fountain pens, and so it proved to be. The replies I received from poetry magazines were written on compliments slips by The Editor, an avuncular but testy figure who might send a few encouraging words written in a discouraging hand.

My poems were always clearer to me when they came back, sometimes painfully so. It was as if their leaving the house had undomesticated them and they no longer had an automatic place among my work. There were a few I grew to trust and when those ones came back to me, I didn't hesitate to send them out again.

—

A poet friend and I used to have a running joke about how whatever she or I wrote about – the formulation of empiricism, the cult of a saint, civil war – our work would be described by critics as 'lyrical' and 'domestic'. This did not make us laugh.

Lyrical suggests a sweet voice and a small song. Domestic, a small subject. (Domesticity is a matter of life and death but it usually occurs quietly within small rooms.)

I was all the more angry because to some extent the critics were right. My poems were sweeter and smaller than I liked to think.

I did not yet understand the true nature of historical foreground and background, that they did not arrange themselves but had been chosen. The missing epic heroic of women was not just that they did work of equal importance but that they did the same work and it was not seen.

—

I studied the Bauhaus at school: Walter Gropius's theories of design, Josef Albers's *Interaction of Color* and Marcel Breuer's tubular-steel chairs. I don't remember a single woman's name being mentioned. Years later, when I visited the Bauhaus archive in Berlin, everything that seemed most inventive and delightful had been made by a woman. The Bauhaus, a fulcrum of modernist design, claimed that it was open to 'any person of good repute, without regard to age or sex', but Gropius thought that women were less able than men to think in three dimensions. When Anni Albers joined in 1922 she was, like most female students, directed towards the textiles department. She took the craft of weaving into the heart of the modernist project and asserted its potential as art.

The thing that strikes you first about Albers's work is its vitality. Her engagement with colour is every bit as exhilarating and investigatory as that of her husband, for whom she was a vital collaborator. Every piece asks questions about image, depiction, material, pattern, rhythm, sensation. Close up, you can see how this vitality is inextricable from adventure and intelligence. Her work has the conviction that comes from an artist who has chosen to depend only on herself:

    . . . most important to one's own growth is to see oneself
    leave the safe ground of accepted conventions and to find

oneself alone and self-dependent. It is an adventure which can permeate one's whole being.[4]

For me, writing is a cycle of building safe ground and then leaving it and finding myself alone and eventually becoming permeated by the adventure to the extent that new ground emerges.

Albers worked in complex geometric abstractions but also made 'pictorial weavings' that are poised on the cusp of image. She explored every aspect of what she was doing, experimenting with floating threads and the visual pull of meandering lines. She studied the theory of knots and numerical sequencing in nature. Her diploma project was a stage curtain made of cellophane and chenille which absorbed sound and reflected light. She used grass, lurex and horsehair, and made a necklace of corks and hairpins. There is an epic work of Holocaust memorial as well as a tiny study of pure texture made from the raised bumps of pinpricks in paper.

Such artists routinely turn out to be more radical than the men around them. Withheld from the centre, misinterpreted, unaffirmed and dis-equipped, they have to be. Every time I go to a show of such work, I come out feeling a mixture of triumph and rage.

16. This is my voice

> . . . that load, that weight, that gnawing conscience, that
> sea which to drink up, that frightful task . . . Did anyone
> realize what discipline and self-control it cost him to shape a
> sentence or follow out a hard train of thought?
>
> Thomas Mann[5]

There are many stories in which a man or a god tries to drink
up the sea. Thor did it inadvertently when challenged to empty
a drinking horn whose tip rested in the ocean. The best-known
version is Nietzsche's analogy for the loss of faith in 'The Parable
of the Madman':

> How could we drink up the sea? Who gave us the sponge to
> wipe away the entire horizon? What were we doing when we
> unchained this earth from its sun? Whither is it moving now?
> Whither are we moving? Away from all suns?[6]

In 'A Weary Hour', one writer (Mann) imagines another
(Schiller), a hundred years earlier, working at night. A hundred years later, I lie awake thinking of Mann – so troubled,
indulged, gifted and exhausting. It's true that writing is a terrible task. Among the arts, it is unusually direct, solitary and
abstract. A writer, of all artists, must hold their nerve.

I start in formlessness. I must go to sea and take it in.

But the capacity to drink up the sea, to accommodate what needs to be written and all that brings it into being, is an act of dismantlement. I dismantle everything I know about the world and how writing works and what it should look and sound like. I take in something shapeless and limitless so that it becomes my self. The discipline comes first – holding my nerve. I embody the sea and I wait. I need to believe that I have the capacity to contain an idea as it connects to a thousand others. However much of a contortion this might be, however bloated or grotesque or grandiose, I must determine that I can contain it. I must believe in the world I conjure, even though no one else can enter it until it is complete.

I also have to drink up the long silence of the women who stood among these men, whose work was made small and who lent to men their own capacities.

I drink all this up and I write and wait till I find myself in a place where it seems no one has been before. I need to feel that I have discovered something. It may be that I've been there already but have forgotten this. Just now I went to make a note on a book I've been circling for years, and one day hope to write, only to find I made the exact same note a year ago. I knew and I didn't know. I remembered and I forgot. Writing depends on this movement, on drinking up and then forgetting what it is you have been drinking.

—

I was at a festival in Sweden that was held out of term-time at a remote teacher-training college. There were writers from all over the world and a large Swedish audience, and we all stayed there together. There was nothing nearby, no town or bar, and the writers would set out in teams in search of one of the government-run alcohol stores. Each night, the director decided in the moment who was to read next and so the stress of being about to go on stage was doubled by not knowing when. It felt like school and we formed gangs and mine included a Finnish writer, who was also a jazz pianist. The last time we'd met, I'd sung with him. The Swedish festival director had been there too and so now on the last evening, when they put a PA and a piano in a marquee, he said *Please, you two, perform for us again*.

A Mexican author sang first and I could tell that she had a good voice but that the PA was terrible. It blunted every syllable and made her sound like someone shouting at a wall. The pianist beckoned me and I knew that I would sound terrible too but picked up the mic. *It's only polite*. He set off in an impossible key, my throat tightened and the words were gone but I couldn't step back. I tried to sing. As my voice failed, the audience laughed and started to sing instead. Suddenly, it was school, where I'd learnt what happened to girls who step forward and say *I can do this* and *Listen to me*. Afterwards, the kind Australian writer said that I'd made *a brave attempt* and the director said something in Swedish that got a huge laugh. I asked for a translation. *He described you as sometimes a good singer*. They were all straightforwardly amused and forgot it the next minute but I was furious with myself. Had I learnt nothing? Years after the band, I was still abandoning myself to failure rather than saying *No* or *Yes, but only like this.*

To be sometimes a good singer means that you have a voice but you aren't taking charge of it. You're allowing others to determine the sound you make – even when they don't intend to – by not paying attention to what a voice requires. You also need to be at ease with your desire to sing in the first place.

It would be easy to explain myself in terms of my lack of presence. *I wasn't there* (*again*). But that would be to overlook something that still makes me uncomfortable. I wanted to sing just as I wanted to join a conversation or express my ideas. I had been taught to speak softly and not to demand attention, but here I was, being quite loud, a bit harsh and very off-key. I did not know what to do with the seriousness, force and ambition of my intention, and so I offered it up as a joke.

—

But who can really hear the sound they make? I came into writing knowing nothing of the literary world. I was told what my writing was and accepted the description I was given. I was called a poetess which was corrected to woman poet which was corrected to poet although I still meet people who call me a poetess.

Three adjectives have often been used to describe my poetry: cool, intelligent, precise. All poetry should be intelligent and precise but what of this so-called coolness? Is there something about how I comport myself that is not sufficiently friendly? Am I not doing enough to make you comfortable?

How can I keep you warm? Would it be easier for you if I behaved more like your idea of a poetess? If I danced a little too wildly, if my dress slipped from my shoulders. Do you not see me dancing and letting slip in my own way? Must I bleed?

There are those who like poetry written by women as long as it confines itself to their idea of what that should be. These people include women.

A man stands there not dancing. He assumes that those who are dancing don't know when to be still, or how to focus the lens and build the frame. (Why does he tell me about the lens and the frame as if they are not my subjects and instruments?) I was taught to stand still but I've come to know that being unmoved by your subject, not allowing it to rearrange you, not following it back down the dark path, leads only to words.

Sometimes the dancers find me too still because I don't want to let slip for the sake of it.

The coolness in my poetry is not only a problem for those who have strong ideas about how I should sound. It's also there because I grew up among the dead white men and took on their habits and tastes. Without knowing it, I had been performing as a male writer. My idea of what was good, serious, valuable and legitimate was the same as that of a European man old enough to be my great-grandfather. His authority is so inherent that it's difficult to gather your own without letting him in. But I will not abandon precision and intelligence, or stop working towards clarity and authority, even as these values need to be reconstituted.

Coolness was also a way to smooth things over – myself, my voice, the poem. I wasn't resisting femininity. I was, once again, perfecting a tablecloth.

> They shook it out and laid it down, smoothing out the folds that made a gentle grid from end to end. The grid surely proved that order prevailed in this house.
>
> Dorothea Tanning[7]

I'm afraid of strong music in writing and how easy it is to rely on it alone, but musical tension drives every word on the page. I know exactly where each stress falls, each beat, and how every cadence is shaped. This means that I know my voice and how I want it to sound but I have still given it up to compromise. When I hear someone else reading my words, not just my poems, I realise that I've been scoring them all along, even when I've written words to be set to music. The first time I worked with a composer, I didn't hear any of the music until the opening night and I had to stop myself leaping to my feet and shouting, *It doesn't go like this!* Later, I worked with a composer who set my words with such insight and precision that I could no longer hear them unsung.

—

I was told to expect a call that week from the man producing one of my books for radio. Two months later, he got in touch. *It's got to be done by next Tuesday*, he said. *You could read it yourself. You've got a nice voice. I can still hear a bit of Essex.* He'd heard me say a handful of words. *I don't think so*, I said, offering four more. I didn't want to give this man my voice to play with. *I'm off on holiday next week*, he said, *so who do you suggest?* He found an actor and directed her to play a one-note bratty adolescent. The production was full of mistakes and mispronunciations, and he got the music wrong. He didn't care, he was off on holiday.

17. Ordinary speech

When women started to talk about their silenced experience, men were offered this advice: *Listen and ask questions*. I watched men huddle together, telling each other stories of witch-hunts and persecutions, of the cartoonish examples that enable them to push the whole thing away. I saw women be complicit in these conversations. Many of the men around me were silent. They did not know what to say and were scared of getting it wrong and of expressing themselves in a way that got them into trouble. In trying to talk about this, we are confounded by the ways in which ordinary speech can itself be a silencing act. It is the ordinariness of the words, our habits in using them, and the ways in which value is bound up with meaning that make this so difficult to overcome.

This has prompted us to consider what we have folded away, including what we cannot bear to remember – the major events and the minor ones too: the daily incursions and distortions, the contaminations and retranslations. Again it is the ordinariness that is so shocking. I was in a queue outside a venue with a single narrow entrance. There were too many people trying to get in and suddenly no one could move. A security guard yelled that everyone should just stand still. There was a man by my left elbow – no more than my height and half my age – who started to speak quietly in my ear. *Look what you've done. You fucking stupid bitch. This is all your fault.* We were so pressed together that I could barely turn my head. There was a woman with him but she couldn't hear. I could feel his breath on my skin as he whispered on and on. *See what you've done? You fucking selfish fucking ignorant bitch.* He was smiling as he said it, not at me but to himself. When we were allowed to move, I attempted to tell someone who worked there about this (he was caught up in trying to control the crisis, he said: *How is this helping me right now?*) when a colleague of his darted over flapping her hands and speaking in a baby voice – *Oo I don't like this, I'm scared!* While I was making myself sound as level as possible in order to be heard, she had seen me claim his attention and competed for it by giving a performance of a frightened girl.

Speech is of the body, and language that has been made by men is of the male body. Women are taught from the start to imitate or defer to the male body if they want to enter male terrain – that is if they want to be taken seriously. What imbues seriousness? Being able to objectify is not the same as being objective.

A woman who works in corporate finance boasted to me of playing the woman and playing the man. This is not how she described it. She seemed unaware of the caricatures she was acting out when she described how, when a female colleague was distressed, *I do all that you know all that there there, give her a hug, all that. Then I get back to work.* When she spoke of the boardroom, she started to punctuate her sentences with 'fuck'. *You have to be so fucking strong to stay in that room,* she said, *really strong to be taken fucking seriously and I can do that.* I wanted to ask what she understood by *strong* and *serious* but I said nothing. Her body has started to be at war with itself. Her hair is falling out. She's finding it difficult to breathe.

I had a job where a man fifteen years older than me, who wasn't promoted to my grade and who worked to my direction, refused to engage with paperwork or follow procedure. When I decided to leave, he started sending me hate mail *to clear the air*. He complained both that I had never had lunch with him and that I had not been a colleague but *only* his boss. He said that I believed that I did the *real work*. I did. But I wrote back patiently addressing each point he made as if they were worth proper consideration, as if he would listen and change his mind. He sent back one line – *You are deluded*. I was not only disappointing but mad.

His messages did not invite a response. They were the waste products of a man relieving some internal pressure. He couldn't be bothered to do the boring bits because at home his wife ran everything despite her own vocation. He could drop things where they fell and move on, confident that someone would clear up. The place where we worked was so dysfunctional that I knew there was no point in going to my manager or making a complaint. The only thing that marked my departure, apart from his messages, was an email notifying me of the deletion of my email account. *Why can't you just be nice?*

—

I was at a classical concert where the programme started with something pretty and familiar. It was a summer afternoon, at a festival, and the atmosphere was sleepy and genial. People had had *a nice walk and a good lunch*. In the second half, the curtain

111

opened on an acid-pink dimpled latex backdrop. This was the set for the final piece – a song cycle based on the hallucinatory writings of a medieval nun, performed in fetish gear by a soprano who spent most of her time twisting on the floor. Before that came a short work for wind ensemble. This proved to be far more of a shock.

The players sat in a semicircle in front of the pink dimples. They raised their instruments to their lips and then made almost no sound. There was enough substance to the sound to control the silence but it refused to become music. The tension in the players' bodies as they gathered themselves to make noise and then cut themselves off was difficult to bear. The piece was not long but it felt interminable as the tension moved from the stage to the audience. As we tried to listen we were met with our own need for silence to be filled. Among four hundred strangers sitting close together, this unease was hard to contain. I became increasingly aware of my body and willed it not to make any noise. As the piece developed but withheld itself, the audience started to lose control. Men of a certain age, those who comfortably fill a seat, began to cough or sneeze and then to yelp and bark. These were split-second, concentrated emissions that had been held back for as long as possible. They couldn't bear the discomfort in their bodies that this tension produced.

In my need to silence my own body, I amplified theirs. I have no idea who they were but hold them in my mind as lost boys. They were sent away to a school which separated them not only from family but from their bodies. Rarely alone, they were exposed, scrutinised and mocked, and survived this through disconnects. At odds with their bodies, with their own desires, they become rigid and unresponsive. They refuse to moderate themselves. *What's your problem?* They coddle their bellies and don't bother to do up their flies. They revel in their physical decay while not quite believing that it's happening. They waggle their penises to indicate that they want sex. They think they're *free and easy* and *without hang-ups* but they fuck with desperation, not seeking contact, only release, and they cut off from those who provide it in case they're made to feel. The hardest thing to bear is feeling. It sits on them like slime.

18. Echo

For a long time, I didn't dare sound like myself. I didn't know how to. I read and read and wanted to talk back to what I read but how to speak and what to say? All I could do was mimic the voice that was speaking to me, like Echo: 'that talkative nymph who cannot stay silent when another speaks'.[8]

Echo 'was fond of talking, and whether in chat or argument, would have the last word'.[9] She talks as a form of arrest, detaining Juno, the suspicious wife of Jupiter, to give him time to slip away from compromising situations. Talk of this kind is not about drawing attention to the self (Echo isn't competing for Jupiter's interest) so much as about testing your power of connection.

Perhaps that's why I was so talkative as a child. I lived in fear of someone I loved disappearing and didn't believe that my presence was enough to hold their attention, let alone entice them to return. I had to offer something beyond myself, to entertain. But if you 'cannot stay silent while another speaks', you aren't listening. It is not a conversation and so no real connection can be made.

Juno is angry with Echo because her ploy works. The goddess is detained by nothing more than 'chat or argument' and her erring husband eludes her. She curses Echo who, from that point, can utter only the last words someone else has said.

> . . . she cannot begin
> to speak: her nature has forbidden this;
> and so she waits for what her state permits:
> to catch the sounds that she can then give back
> with her own voice.[10]

She cannot begin and yet she is where we all begin. We only really set out in ourselves when we find our own voice, and speak first, but we begin by repeating what is said to us, even before we understand what it means.

How to end? Echo insists on having the last word (she cannot help it) but takes those words from the other. This denies the separation between what you say and I say – something we depend upon in order to make sense.

Echo is often depicted with her hands raised or clutching at her head or with her cloak pulled across her face. She is dominated by landscape, held back by the trees, confused with other figures. The weather is fine, if a little dull. The air is clear and still. Nothing moves. Her body wastes away, leaving only her bones, and when they are gone she exists purely as voice. There is no freedom in this. Consider the acoustics. She needs confinement and obstruction in order to be heard at all and so has to live in mountains, caves and cliffs. What if no one speaks? Will she feel relieved or obliterated?

Her greatest torment comes when she desires Narcissus, who senses someone among the trees and calls out, 'Who's here?' and Echo can only answer, 'Here!' He cries, 'Come!' and she can't help but oppose him with her own command, 'Come!' This inadvertent stand-off persists as Narcissus asks, 'Why do you shun me?' and Echo can only offer back his question.[11] Narcissus is repelled by Echo, probably because she makes no sense. She is also unable to answer any question. She can reveal nothing. When she approaches he cries out, 'I would die before I would have you touch me!' What else can she say but, 'I would have you touch me'?[12]

She is so humiliated by this that she withdraws into isolation.

> . . . she hides within the woods;
> there she, among the trees, conceals her face,
> her shame; since then she lives in lonely caves.[13]

Her unintended declaration – *I would have you touch me* – may be shaming but it is also the truth. Echo desires Narcissus. Ovid compares her to sulphur brought close to a flame. Through the upsetting of language and the introduction of strange laws, through reflexive reiteration, we arrive at an unspeakable truth. She is a struck match.

Narcissus gives Echo no more thought than anyone else who has declared an interest in him. Gripped by his own reflection in a pool, he too wastes away because he is unable to make contact, only in his case it is with himself. It is said that when he died, Echo 'took up his sigh'[14] – *Alas!* It might sound as if agency has been restored to her and she is choosing to express pity. But isn't her echo of his 'alas' as meaningless as anything else she now says? She has not chosen the words.

There are times when we can only echo those around us but other people's words may help us to shape our own. We cannot make direct contact with ourselves, not even in reflection, and so depend upon other voices, other songs, to access our deepest feelings. For Echo, there are only other songs: 'The wood nymphs mourned him too, and Echo sang her refrain from their lament.'[15] She is simplified into sound, existing in air, perceived only as the reflex she cannot help but perform.

—

When a man repeats what a woman says – a witticism, an insight, an idea – he may be heard when she has not been. He becomes her voice and she becomes his echo, though the words she's echoing are her own. This story takes place in the days when business was done on paper and by telephone. A woman I once knew who might have been me received a box containing the proofs for her next book. They came with a friendly note. Underneath the proofs was a second set with another note, intended for the book's proofreader. *Don't bother reading this against the original. A quick look-through will do.* The note went on: *Well here it is, a pale imitation of the poet himself.* The poet was the person she lived with. She was being described as his echo.

She rang the man who'd written the note and told him that she'd received the parcel and that it had included the proofreader's set. He asked her to return them to him to be redirected. She said that he had also included his note to the proofreader. He asked her to return that too. *Do you remember what that note said?* she asked. He didn't and so she read it to him. (She became his echo.) He ended the conversation, only to call back half an hour later to apologise. It was one of those apologies that delete themselves as they go along. *I'm sorry if you felt* . . . She didn't care what this man thought of her poems. She told him that she knew he couldn't be expected to admire every book that crossed his desk but that he should treat them with equal respect. He clearly felt not only that she had no voice of her own but that her work was not worth proper care and attention.

Was she a pale imitation? As soon as she was with *the poet himself*, people no longer trusted that she had her own voice. (They also cast her as his secretary, her own friends even, asking her to pass on invitations and messages years after they had split up.) To some extent they were right. He had taken control of the rooms and the books so why not of what could be said? Her work retreated. Not because he had a hand in it but because there was so little room for her inner life in their life. She couldn't be herself or use her own words. If she offered correction to his words, which no one imagined she might need to, or if she showed that she knew something he didn't, there was an explosion. So she dared not say words beyond his and yes, she existed in pale imitation. Rather than lose her voice completely, she existed in echo.

19. Formative

When my first book appeared in 1993, I was described as a poet who writes about science. I've never said this of myself but it is how I have been summarised. It became the thing to ask me about alongside being a woman poet.

I didn't choose my subject matter, I followed my curiosity. There are poems about radium, artificial insemination and photography in that book but there are also plenty of sunsets and seas. If anything, I announce my themes as water, weather and light. I wrote those poems through my twenties – before I'd had a formal, public response and with little sense of what my influences or imperatives might be. Now I was being told. It seemed that my work was making claims for itself and I was expected to defend them. I started to doubt my relationship with what I wrote.

When I was at school, science was chalk on blackboard with the occasional excitement of something fizzing over a Bunsen burner or the chance to dissect a bull's eye. My chemistry report said that, *despite professing an antipathy for science, Lavinia has some ability.* I was evidently vocal about how boring I found it. But science, and medicine in particular, was what I grew up with. Throughout my childhood, my father ran a dispensing practice. We were guinea pigs for the mixtures he prepared, being asked to comment on an excess of peppermint oil or synthetic banana. Meals were dominated by lively debates about tapeworm or yeast infections. We were offhand about the reflected glory of being related to the person who answered the call at the cinema, service station or ice rink for *a doctor in the house*. Once when we were queuing in a cafeteria to pay for our food, my father saw that a man was about to have an epileptic fit and seemed to leap over tables and fly through the air to be immediately beside him. The phone would ring in the middle of the night and he'd be halfway dressed and grabbing his bag as he answered it. At school, friends would ask my advice on their injuries and I developed a convincing bedside manner. There were anatomical charts in the garden shed, ampoules of heroin in a locked cupboard and books about sexual technique on the study shelf.

Like the children of actors or soldiers, we were expected to follow in our parents' footsteps, although they withheld any expectations just as they withheld their fears. My siblings trained in chemistry, engineering and astrophysics. At sixteen I was reading Shakespeare, Beckett and Eliot, and trying to think about space and time. My brother the astrophysicist, who also studied philosophy and wrote poetry, patiently answered my questions about the cosmos and I started to understand why I was not a scientist. Nor was I a philosopher. Like Hamlet and his friends, we were students having late-night conversations after the pub had shut, trying out big ideas under the guise of banter. With Hamlet in mind, I said that if you free yourself of the human scale, there is only futility. My brother replied that if it is futility, you cannot be free of the human scale. In thinking about the human need not to see further, I'd done that exact thing. I later had a dream in which I called out to my brother, *I can't see anything in this mist*, and he called back, *Then open your eyes!*

That mist is my subject. I am absent-minded, deeply interior and have a poor sense of direction. Life is punctuated by moments when I have no idea where I am or what's in front of me. I can't see, I can't understand what's being said or I can't make sense. This is my 'science' and what I write about.

My brother borrowed a telescope plate from his lab to help explain things to me. He pointed to a few of the white specks: *There's a galaxy and there's a galaxy . . .* And this was only a six degrees by six degrees portion of the sky. My mind strained and went blank. The next night he went to a party, fell asleep somewhere and mislaid the plate. It was found eventually and he returned it to the lab unnoticed. He also told me about binary star systems which were caught in one another's gravity. I wrote a poem mentioning both the stars and the telescope plate, which was broadcast on the radio. They happened to be listening in his lab that afternoon and were pleased to hear a poet writing about stars but he didn't get to borrow any more plates.

I started to refer to my subject as perception and then as interrupted perception. Perhaps it is just plain interruption. Writing and thinking come alive when something snags – I can't make sense or find the words, there's a rupture in the flow of the mind, a pause in the drive to process what it's perceiving and to turn it into what it already knows. I am trying to find an expressive structure that puts in place the experience of being out of place.

During his research, my brother went to work at an observatory in Australia. Freak weather brought the first rain for

121

decades. He couldn't see the stars so instead he watched flowers appear from seeds that had lain dormant all that time. I wrote about the desert and the flowers and got excited about time. I also wrote about how the keeper of Big Ben used to stack old pennies on the pendulum to slow the clock into accommodating the extra seconds in the year, and how racing pigeons were thrown off course when a solar flare disrupted the Earth's magnetic field. Perhaps I was drawn to such stories because of their homeliness, their anecdotal cosiness. They were charming (so lyrical, so domestic!). I disguised the seriousness of my intentions, as I had learnt to do, and wrote my poems as if they were just another of the conversations we had when walking back from the pub.

Men wrote me letters correcting what they perceived to be my ideas about science. I took part in panels with scientists who were either dismissive, highly literate and keen to talk, or eager to read me poems of their own. Those open to conversation have helped me extend and shape my thinking – which is not to say that I understand more about science. I have been invigorated by encountering such difference in method, value, expression and deduction while discovering shared imperatives too.

People assume that a poet is 'poetic', by which they mean instinctive, subjective and vague. Placing the scientist in opposition to this casts them as objective, logical and precise. There are times when a poet must be rigorous and exact, and a scientist imaginative and instinctive. Great scientific discoveries have been made in dreams. Great poems are those in which the most nebulous aspects of experience are rendered clear through the activation and orchestration of language at the deepest level.

Of course each goes by different laws and has a different aim in mind but both the arts and the sciences are more than ever bound up with the variables and limitations of human perception. Poetic freedoms can be used to express scientific ideas in a more broadly comprehensible manner and can locate them within the ultimately human context by which science is driven and defined. The human experience of science remains a human one. Science depends upon storytelling to explain itself. I was on a panel with a chemist whose starting point was that he had no use for metaphor. *How do you describe what you see?* I asked him. *And why do you name what you see? Why not just give everything numbers?*

When my brother was finishing his doctorate, a study of the spectra of a particular cluster of stars, I asked him what progress he had made. He said it had been a good month because he had got a result. What was it? *Twenty thousand light years plus or minus twenty thousand light years.* I may not be able to make sense of this but I accept it as a cancelling-out, an ultimate conclusion.

After the response to my first book, I talked too much about how science was not my subject. I think now that I was unnerved to have felt such a strong pull towards something, and to have got so excited. When asked the science question, I would say something about how science was mostly too seductive, incomprehensible and exciting to be anything other than borrowed. It was as if I'd come to the end of a difficult romance and the real hurt lay in how susceptible I had been. I was admitting that I'd been seduced and I was ashamed of this.

But a subject ought to be exciting and I ought to feel seduced. I was unnerved to realise how strongly poetry operated within me and had no idea what compelled me. I wrote to find out.

20. Talking about myself

We were trained never to talk about ourselves.
But what if someone asked you about yourself?
They never did.

The questions I've been asked most often are the hardest to answer. People ask about inspiration and routine as if they are recipes I should be willing to share. For the first decade of my writing life, they asked me about being a woman poet.

Let's now talk about your experience as a woman poet.
Only if we can also talk about your experience as a male poet.
But it's important to address femininity in your work.
And to address masculinity in yours – to address them both in my work and yours.

I never sounded as confident as this. I managed a few times to say something like the above but with a great deal of blushing and demurral.

People asked questions as a way of telling me who I was and what I wrote about. I did my best to come up with a reply. If someone asked something stupid, I might contort my answer so as not to give their stupidity away. If they were aggressive, I became possessed of extreme good manners, which made me feel later as if I had slightly poisoned myself, which I had. I'd dismissed myself, making jokes about what I wrote and being offhand about what poetry should be and can do.

The man in the extrovert suit bounded over to me in the green room. He talked about how delighted he was to be chairing my event, how much he had enjoyed the book and how he had so many questions. He was looking neither at me nor at my book. Five minutes later, he was introducing me on stage and got as far as my first name before going blank. He read my surname off the front of the book and then turned it over and read the blurb on the back. And still I thanked him afterwards.

Just before I went on stage, a man sauntered up to me in the wings of the theatre and said he was there to interview me. He liked doing it because he got a free pass to the festival, and access to the food and drink in the green room. What was my book called and what questions would I like him to ask? On stage, he asked me to explain what I just had. He wasn't listening.

A critic being thoughtful about what I do and examining it carefully is far more satisfying than praise. There's a useful response that points to a difficulty you knew was there but couldn't pinpoint. I don't mind if they conclude that a book doesn't quite work. I never think they work. I also don't mind being told what they're about. I only find out what I've written about a year or two after a book is published, so for a while I don't know how to talk about it. I'm making it up.

There are also those who say they don't understand (oh modern poetry!) and this is not an invitation to explain. They want you to know that your work is difficult but they also approach it in a state of refusal. They ask *What is this about?*

and every time I take that as a serious invitation. They point to a page and say *I don't know what this means!* And the fault is not with them, it is with the page. They look at me expectantly. I am supposed to solve this. Should I apologise on behalf of some other poet? Or should I go along with what this person is pretending to say and offer to help him understand it? Whatever I say, it is bound to be clever-clever and to involve far too many words.

I was at a festival event chaired by the books editor of a prominent journal. By way of greeting, he told me how difficult he found my work. We offered each other quick smiles as if to agree that this was not going to be a problem. When he introduced me on stage, he described me as *terribly serious, probably lonely and a bit sad.* I read poems about getting drunk and dancing. This time, my interviewer was ready with his questions.

I don't understand your poems, he said. *Why don't you want people to understand them? I mean, not even you understand them, do you, you say so right here!* He opened my book and prodded at a line while reading it out triumphantly: *'Why did I choose not to understand?'*

It's a line in a poem not something I said, I thought (but didn't say). *You do know what a poem is, don't you? Because I'm beginning to wonder.*

He was elated, smiling hard, leaning forward on the edge of his chair, excited at last to be able to exercise his putdown. *You say it right here – you choose not to understand your own poems.*

Did my book make you feel a bit stupid? I didn't say. *Are you punishing me for that?*

Even after this, I tried to respond as if he had asked me an acceptable question. At one point a member of the audience intervened to complain about how he was attacking me. When I was signing books afterwards, he came up with his copy and said *You'll probably write 'fuck off' in this but then maybe it'll be worth a lot of money one day.*

Fuck off, I thought, as I signed it.

21. A woman I once knew who might have been me

Like the growth of crystals: a formative will and the impossibility of adopting any other mode.

Francis Ponge[16]

Writing is an act of separation. I write because I have become separated. I'm attempting to connect in a form from which I will separate. The work succeeds when it becomes separate.

I write in order to meet myself. I want to catch up with, and become, the person I once was and sometimes am and who has always been there – noting what I really think and feel, see and believe.

I would like her to become the only one who speaks.

Our meeting is easily imagined. I make false connections with myself every day.

'He thinks with me,' Dorothea says about Casaubon in *Middlemarch*. It's the moment she, and the reader, understand what draws her to him. He doesn't, of course. She's aligning herself with the movement of his mind and feels the relief of being borne along, of not thinking alone.

If we were looking at something – a view or a painting – he would clamp his arm round my shoulders and point. He became angry if I did not exactly follow his gaze.

'All gathers in incredible joy. I cannot stop writing poems. They come better and better,' wrote Sylvia Plath to her mother about Ted Hughes.[17] 'They come from the vocabulary of woods and animals and earth that Ted is teaching me.' Plath's is not a poetry of vocabulary. Perhaps Hughes described her to herself just when she needed this. She took on his naming of things as a form of confidence but when it came to writing her poems, she set it aside. She was other to him and he to her and they knew they must each move to protect that.

They recognised each other and he said *Show me*, and she found that she could and that for once she was revealing her deep self to someone who met her with recognition and capacity and who renamed what he found as the best of herself, and she said *Follow me*, and he did, all the way down. How to get back? Perhaps each assumed that the other knew the way.

She knew that she was making something of her own that needed to be in proximity to, but not in direct contact with, her husband. 'My poems sprout about him like shoots; even as he goes, I shall go on, for what I have learned in loving him is part of me, now, and not dependent on him; this is the core of my joy.'[18]

The joy of separation, of realising that at the core there is something entirely your own. And then that the poem becomes its own.

H.D. knew not to accept Ezra Pound: 'Ezra would have destroyed me and the centre they call "Air and Crystal" of my poetry.'[19]

The electrification of the other, the one who thinks with me. To learn from them, to take from them but not to become them (or an echo of them).

To protect the centre as crystal and air.

Even as he goes, I shall go on.

The impossibility of adopting any other mode.

22. Venus (a manifesto)

They say Venus stepped onto land new-made and that Venus arrived already a thousand years old. Across the sea. From the east. On a ram or a shell. No matter the vehicle.

Not beginning but finding.

What happens when you place what you've glimpsed in tension.

Venus was born of foam, of movement catching hold of matter. Wave after wave turning over what is too small to be seen. To the point of water catching hold of air. The sea making room.

This could not occur in clear water.

You have to give up being visible, even to yourself, but you must remain present throughout. Unattached and unanchored, you are making room.

It is not enough to valorise agitation. Do not abandon the power of speech. While dismantling its constructs, grasp its matter. Protect the true nature of all you encounter.

Occupy the sacred wood. It is a space between devotion and

135

determination. Fight against taking root while drawing on forces buried underfoot.

Resist values formed out of exclusion but do not resist values that lead to the production of art.

Pay attention to those who are leaving. The morning star and evening star are after all the same thing.

Venus is formed in suspension. A planet turning leisurely in the other direction. A planet draped in cloud. Hidden but not withheld.

You were taught to fold. Use those skills as you unfold.

Do not let the rush into language become an evasion of meaning. Take hold. Tease out all you have absorbed. Take your time in releasing it. Wait till it grows light.

Venus has been depicted more than any other of the divine realm and is intended to be viewed from every angle. Take charge of depiction. Intend every angle.

This is not a performance but it is learnt through performance.

Give way but do not let go. Take charge of what you did not know you know.

Venus is an act of love. Yes, this is of the body.

Learn the difference between truth and certainty. Venus's name is without gender. Venus's father concealed his children in the earth. He was not a father. Venus has no mother. Or a mother that was a version of a father. Who is not Venus's father.

Use other names. Use meaning and the seed of meaning. Do not choose between love and desire. Go deeper. Through noun into verb into gesture.

Venus arose from within (wave after wave).

Commit to resistance as a continuous action, which means that you must act. It is not enough to react.

Honour those whose absence and silence command us to take nothing for granted.

First we must gather and name our terms and make noise. Then we must each find our own voice.

Honour the small words and know that you will not be quiet even as they call you quiet.

Fuck quiet.

23. The rain

It has to do more and at the moment I can't make it do more.
It's better not to look for the words when you can only find
the wrong ones.

I made this note when I was in my twenties and came across it
recently just as I slipped into the same state. I was young and
comforting myself by converting a problem into wisdom, but
the difficulty remains.

I have insight to offer but it is for other people. That writing
can stop working and although this is a shock every time, it is
usually part of a cycle. It happens when you get ahead of yourself. You hurry off towards the next thing without having laid
the ground and you suddenly become aware that you are not
yet equipped. It's like realising that you've run off a cliff and
only then starting to fall. This is when silence steps forward to
meet you. In a strange way, silence carries you across the void.
You have to trust that the work will continue to evolve. It is out
of sight but it will reappear. You will have a new place to stand.
The silence will end – and all this will come round again.

I sit there and try to write, not knowing where I'm going but
waiting for what usually happens: something to gather static,
to surprise me. On a good day, I reach towards an idea and it
reaches back. When this doesn't happen, I feel locked out of
myself as I did at fifteen. There is a room in my head that I

can no longer enter. Worse than that, I can't believe I was ever inside the room or that I was once able to bring writing about.

There are times of deeper silence when I cannot think, let alone write. This is not a fruitful pause in which something is imminent (or immanent). It's a blank surface that doesn't even translate into space. All the 'untidy activity' that usually 'continues awful but cheerful'[1] has ceased. That is the engine noise – the perpetual turning over of stuff that feels progressive and constructive even when nothing's being formed. The engine stops and I lose the feel of the world and a way to describe it. Words go dark. As soon as I touch language, the lights go off.

At such times I am back in the forest, in its darkest parts where there is nothing to hear. I've come to trust that the untidy activity of investigating, connecting, translating and describing persists but so far back in the dark that I have no sense of it happening. Is this the same forest where I get so lost? I think it might be. The more I learn about how writing works, the more I respect the aspects of it that I can only protect rather than deploy. Getting lost in the dark is one of them.

The pull inwards is at its most powerful when I can't write because it can't get hold of something and settle down to work. Any outward movement feels exhausting and days pass as I turn away from completing the most basic action. I can't sustain the focus required to finish a sentence, let alone pick something up off the floor. Nothing tastes of anything and nothing feels. I can't, I just can't.

The room I'm shut out of is the work I have finished, not the work to come. I'm waiting there in the forest for the wherewithal of my next home to appear.

In desperate times, I can find myself in the new room I've been waiting for when I just needed to get away and wasn't thinking about writing at all.

Perhaps I started to write in order to ensure that I had somewhere else to go. Reading showed me how. It's an experience of finding yourself simultaneously elsewhere and travelling your own nature. It is also the enactment of a desire to be quiet. The book in your hands gives you permission to remain silent and alone. How much reading time is spent dreaming?

After my father died, I came across pictures he took of us in the woods, playing in a den that we'd made out of branches. He was a good photographer who knew where to place himself so that we were not aware of his presence. There we are, busy at our work. It was a serious business. There was no domestic role play or story being acted out: the point was to build. We were thorough in the selecting and ordering of branches, that was the game. I don't think we even spent much time inside.

When I'm able to work, I'm not particularly orderly. A lot of time is spent circling and deferring, wandering about and gathering branches.

Most of my homes have been badly converted spaces in worn-out buildings which become metaphors – the roof that loosened and leaked, the dry rot and rubble beneath the floorboards, the cupboard doors that warped and would not close, the blocked drains and short circuits, the dust and moths, the stains and cracks. The place where I have felt most at home is not a house. I am the first human to inhabit it and the animals are still there outside the window as well as in the walls and roof and under the floor. It is an airy space of intimate dimensions which fills up with the outside world. I do not let the rain in but I open the windows to it.

It's not just a question of having a room but of knowing that I can stay there as long as I need to and that if I stand up, go to get food, wander down the street and back again, I won't be interrupted, I am still inhabiting that room. This is difficult to say because I'm making a claim for the specific nature of what I do. I am driven to write and feel desperate when separated from my work but I will still too easily capitulate to other demands.

The writer (if they're lucky) has a room, perhaps even a study. Others have an office, an operating theatre, a laboratory or a studio, which are entered quite differently. They have doors with passcodes and 'No Entry' signs. People understand that what happens inside them is not to be disturbed.

When will you finish? How long will it take? For the first time I don't feel obliged to come up with an answer such as *Around six* or *In time for lunch*. Instead I tell the truth. *I don't know.* I realise that this isn't helpful and worry about sounding self-important and so I backtrack only to arrive at *This is so fucking important!* I don't mean me or even my book but being able to work at the highest level I can. It's not about putting the hours in but rather sustaining a pitch of focus and orchestration. No one is stopping me working but I've felt the need to amplify the situation in this way in order to convince myself. I'm shouting at myself. Lately I've taken to shouting about art.

—

For the rain it raineth every day.
Shakespeare[2]

I have never experienced uninterrupted writing time. Who has unless they have someone to run life for them? Even when my daughter was grown-up and I was able to go and sit on a Swiss mountain or by the Baltic or, best of all, could just stay at home free from any external demands, life moved in to fill whatever space had been created. I was given a grant that would enable me to work on whatever I wanted for three years and decided to give up a job that was anyway making me ill. My child was by now supporting herself. I had a settled life and what felt like a proper home. So I entered this unexpected room and its luxurious, underwritten emptiness. Only life followed. My father reappeared, demented and alone. He was unable to ask for help and so staged emergencies from which we had to rescue him. The lives of those around me were also fraught with emergencies. But I want life and other people in it. And I want to rescue them.

In my early twenties, when writing moved from the background to the foreground of life, I read *Silences*, Tillie Olsen's deeply literary consideration of why women do not get their writing done. It was originally a talk given in 1962, the year that I was born.

I think of Rilke who said, 'If I have any responsibility, I mean and desire it to be responsibility for the deepest and innermost essence of the loved reality [writing] to which I am inseparably bound' . . . he is explaining why he will not take

142

a job to support his wife and baby, nor live with them (years later will not come to his daughter's wedding nor permit a two-hour honeymoon visit lest it break his solitude where he awaits poetry).

Tillie Olsen[3]

Born to Russian revolutionaries in Nebraska in 1912, Olsen had to manage her writing around earning a living, bringing up four daughters and her work as a communist-party activist and campaigner for workers' rights. She didn't finish high school and published her first short story, 'I Stand Here Ironing', at the age of forty three. Although she lived into her nineties, she published only a handful of short stories, her talks and essays, and an unfinished novel.

Rainer Maria Rilke, born in 1875, only just made it to his fifty-first birthday. In roughly half the time given to Olsen, he published nine volumes of poems, a novel (left unfinished 'out of exhaustion'), essays, letters, stories and plays. Friends took him with them to Italy and Russia. He stayed in an artists' colony, maintained a hotel room in southern Spain for over a year and spent a winter in a princess's castle near Trieste. When he was called up during the First World War, friends intervened and he was moved to a desk job. Eventually a patron renovated a schloss in a Swiss valley so that he could have a proper home. I think about his wife (the sculptor Clara Westhoff) and daughter, and roll up my sleeves ready to weigh in alongside Olsen, only to be thrown by her next sentence. 'Extreme – and justified. He protected his creative powers.'

Olsen, too, chose to live alone when she could and eventually did well out of patronage in the form of lecture tours, fellowships, residencies and nine honorary doctorates. She took what she was offered although the time she gained, she appears to have dedicated to educating and encouraging younger writers. Her need to write was subjugated to her commitment to the world that Rilke was so determined to exclude. When she no longer had to do someone's ironing or cook their meals or type their letters or save their jobs, she read their manuscripts. I was surprised to discover that twenty-one years before her first story appeared, Olsen received a substantial advance for a novel that she never delivered. There is a silence about the ways in which she possibly silenced herself when she didn't have to and how this sits within the broader silence of women who have done the same. Perhaps silence was too engrained or too formative to be abandoned as an approach. Life can be a way to avoid writing. One might also suggest that Rilke wrote to avoid his life.

There are great poets who overwhelm themselves and there are a few, like Rilke or Dickinson, who know what lines they must draw around themselves and who have the strength to draw them. Dickinson's life can be seen as a skilful negotiation of freedom and constraint. Her father excused her from morning prayers because he knew she sat up late at night. He didn't ask why. Her parents were tolerant but reserved to the point of emotional absence. This child must have seemed like a volcano (a Dickinson motif) to them.

While she briefly went away to school, Dickinson's education was punctuated by illness. She had a repeated problem with her vision but never wore spectacles. She was not only fragile but susceptible: 'A circus passed the house – still I feel the red in my mind.'[4] This synaesthetic response, in which she is feeling rather than seeing colour, shows how open she was to disarrangement. When the world concentrated itself, she succumbed: '. . . the Chestnut Tree, I met in my walk. It hit my notice suddenly – and I thought the Skies were in Blossom.'[5]

The tapping of the root of the poetic self can be too much for the actual self. In 1862, the year Dickinson reached the height of her productivity, she confesses: 'I had a terror – since September – I could tell to none –'[6] That same year she went through an emotional crisis generally construed as some kind of romantic love. It's clear from her letters and the memories of those who knew her that she was a person of wit and high spirits as well as a passionate and probably exhausting friend. 'The shore is safer . . .' she wrote to her friend Abiah Root, 'but I love to buffet the sea . . . I love the danger!'[7] She found 'ecstasy in living'[8] but kept the world at a distance while undertaking extensive correspondences.

Home was an anchor rather than a shelter. She stayed where she could remain in control of the world, and free from the intrusion of worldly affairs. The space she made in her life in order to be able to live it, and to write, was created and filled by her poems. She gave up much in order to protect it. When Higginson asked her whether refusing society left her in need of something to do, her reply was emphatic:

> I never thought of conceiving that I could ever have the slightest approach to such a want in all future time . . . I feel that I have not expressed myself strongly enough.[9]

145

24. The hard work of sleep

There was a time when I fell in love in a way that was dangerous. It changed my life for good as well as bad and was too much in the end. Some years later, I took a cautious step towards falling in love again. As the idea flickered into life, before I felt anything much, I had a terrifying dream. I woke in its grip but the details evaporated and all I was left with was the feeling of having to make endless urgent decisions. That was all I could remember until, months later, I fell while walking in snow. I took a step and the snow gave way beneath me. It wasn't deep and I only stumbled but I screamed. I made a life-or-death noise because, in that moment, the dream came back to me.

I was out in the city at night, in the rain, near a street corner. A man approached, stepped off the kerb into a puddle and sank without trace. A woman came along and she too stepped into the puddle and sank, only this time her arm rose up out of the water. Someone else appeared, took hold of her hand and was pulled under. It was unclear whether or not anyone surfaced. Another person was walking towards the scene. They would step off the kerb. What should I do?

I was watching it all from across the road as if it were a play, but I also took everyone's part in it. I was the man who disappeared before he had time to realise what was happening to him and the woman trying to surface and the person who was by chance within reach of her hand. I was also myself, able to issue a warning (to myself) but not knowing how. Every aspect of the situation spoke of what I was dealing with and yet I let it go – until I took that particular step and the ground gave way.

The dream had remained with me after all, deep in the dark and no less powerful for having been forgotten. When I fell, I felt the same terror I would had it been an actual memory. Given how dreams construct themselves, it could be said that it was a concentration of memory further intensified by the action having been repeated.

For years afterwards, I kept seeing a woman reaching out and the gesture refracting into every other time she had done the same thing. This was the start of a story that took me more than a decade to write.

Echo could only repeat what others said but we need to repeat ourselves in order to make sense of things and we do so in ways we're not aware of, enacting a question again and again. That's what I'm doing when I write but I try not to repeat my approach. I find ways to interrupt my habitual path but I am travelling the same question.

In recent years, my body has forgotten how to go to sleep. It's never been easy because my mind doesn't trust the idea of slowing down and my body's response is to brace itself against a fall. My dreams are often exhausting. I wake feeling that I have already done the work of that day. I am anyway reluctant to wake up as I find that half-awake state particularly useful. I like to ponder. My mind follows no particular direction but I'm able to take hold of what arises and turn it over. It's something more than a daydream and less than a thought, and seems to be as important as both.

—

I told him that I'd stopped having dreams. *Your life's a dream,* he said.

I write out of the hard work of sleep. Without sleep or dreams, there would not be that long moment of waking.

There is finding the words but there is also drifting, getting lost and staring into space.

I try to wait as long as possible before settling on what I mean.

I move away from the page when writing feels like trying to look directly at bright snow.

Perhaps this is what I write: a dream remembered as I step into snow.

25. What, when, where, why, (who)

(Answers without questions taken from past interviews)

I've been writing since I could write. I can't imagine not writing. I believe if I had never been published I would still be writing. It's my way of translating the world or experience, or a desire to . . . I don't know what it is.

I never imagined being a writer because although I read avidly I never thought I could meet a writer, let alone be a writer. I didn't connect writing with being a writer and I still don't.

I'm inspired by myopia, migraine, weather, absent-mindedness, light, sea, sky, photography, architecture, film, music, anything about to take shape, including an observation, any pattern about to form.

Being a woman poet was not a condition I aspired to but then I didn't want to be a male poet either.

The point is it's not the point, or shouldn't be only it sometimes is anyway and for the wrong reasons.

I put things in my notebooks in order to let them decay – to break down and reveal themselves.

They evolve over years and can sit in drawers for years, often incomplete and mysterious until they meet something that completes and clarifies them.

I like the way poetry acknowledges this fumbling towards sense in the ever-emergent qualities of its language.

I don't expect somebody reading a poem of mine to have the same surface experience.

I was about to say that sound is not independent of meaning, that it is part of meaning, but I'm also aware of how it can create, as you say, a double life.

Rather like being given a key and finding the door it fits years later.

Waking up, making a pot of tea, and not talking to anyone.

A dark-grey wall.

Although writers are particular about their tools, they go about the thing with a certain avertedness which the fancy notebook would pre-empt.

The distances and the struggle to cross them . . . geographical, emotional, linguistic, imaginative, and so on. The horse, the train, the telegraph, wires, plugs, pulleys and ropes are a far more accurate analogy for the variables involved than the fibre-optic or laser beam.

Gulliver. I'm easily unanchored and susceptible to a loss of proportion and scale. I also get lost all the time and do not trust my own eyes.

I found myself allowing for what might be called the miraculous.

The overheard and glimpsed, language that contains itself taking shape: lo-fi, misheard, rough acoustics . . . Being on the road between two lives, dancing as a form of escape, being framed and taking flight.

What never varies is the first feeling – when something goes straight to the back of your head. It's a feeling of acuity and capacity in which connections are made.

And that really is the idea. I mean it's not an idea because an idea has more form than that.

I create an impossible situation for myself.

The pre-verbal sensation of it.

It might never meet the other thing it needs in order to become a poem.

I don't believe in rules or steps, just natural laws which operate differently every time. Each work has its own physics.

I am most open when I'm working in containment.

A rearrangement in order to see the parts?

Interrupted perception and interrupted description.

Something I almost cannot imagine.

How much I am bringing with me when I travel towards something I have never seen.

I think I'm always testing perception as much as its object and that this is something I became conscious of rather than consciously applied . . . I decided long before that that I preferred the idea of things to the actual. Being short-sighted meant that seeing, and making sense of what I saw, was an effort and a volatile and uncertain endeavour.

My first novel grew out of a poem that accidentally became a story. It took me years to find out how to write it. A poem is something you can turn over in your hands whereas a novel is a world you have to travel. I'd say I'm a poet who has written some fiction and may write some more.

I can't answer for the others, but I didn't set out to write a novel.

I didn't intend to write a novel. I was writing a poem about two memories: of jumping through a window and of crossing a frozen and ploughed field at night. All of a sudden I had a character and I could see her clearly and then it wasn't a poem but a story.

I didn't set out to write a novel, I just had a poem in which a character emerged and then a story. Eight years later I'd written a book.

What I mean is I didn't decide to write a novel.

My response to this is to want to discuss what we might mean by 'conceptual' and 'experimental'.

That's an interesting observation. Yes, one kind of wall in this is the wall we build in ourselves – for those questions and answers we need to conceal.

I live on a small island with constantly changing weather. Everything comes down to light and water.

I was hoping it would work as both.

I don't think I'm showing anybody anything they haven't seen before but I am hoping to get them to see it as if they haven't seen it before in order to consider it more deeply.

I didn't so much want to write a book about music as about

music as an agency of experience . . . It was a book about becoming myself and, I finally realised, a book about becoming, and refusing to be, a girl. So the girl part of the equation came last.

What I'm always striving towards is being able, through thought and technique, to create the lightest possible vessel.

I'm trying to create transparency as well.

Yes. You are never taking the same steps in the same sequence into the same place.

After all, words are not supposed to be an end in themselves, are they?

I think I've answered this in the first reply but let me know if you want me to say more.

26. The tree in my heart

I was a young poet for twenty years. I'd sit there, a woman in her forties with a grown-up child, and be introduced as young. This wasn't a compliment. The person saying the words was reading an out-of-date blurb not looking at me.

> Poets are in the beginning hypotheses, in the middle facts,
> and in the end values.
>
> Randall Jarrell[10]

This is still the idea of the poet's trajectory, of all artists perhaps. It's how they are presented and received, and is hard to resist. It's also a young man's trajectory, one who starts out with a passport and time on his hands, grows comfortable and then eminent. I had a child in the middle of my lyric youth and I have never felt as many questions arise as I do now in the factual years of my fifties.

Before I was young, I was new. I had no idea of the possibilities of the literary world, no anticipation or sense of what things might mean. My editor rang up to say I'd been shortlisted for a prize I'd never heard of. Now I meet people who haven't yet published a poem but say their aim is to win that prize. This was in the last years before the internet when most of us emerged blinking out of solitary writing lives and then stumbled towards each other. We took each next step as it appeared and had no sense

155

of this as a career. We were not conscious of what was imposed on us but nor were we conscious of our privilege. There were grants and prizes, invitations and parties, and I was in the room with writers who were calling me a writer too. The joy of it was meeting others whose wiring I recognised. Some have become lifelong friends and others not although they are still of my tribe. We may not like each other much, but we know who we are.

You're in the room but you'll never be new again. This doesn't matter except that what brought you there isn't in the room but back in the dark of your first writing. You'll either settle down to repeat yourself or you'll spend the rest of your years working back towards it.

You're still in the room only now you're furniture. You are visible and perhaps even useful. If you stay long enough, you might become antique. And who are all these people? What are they saying? Why are they all so young?

It is right that the young confound the old. They are good with words in ways we older writers cannot understand unless we are prepared to situate ourselves differently. Their music will grate on our ears and we will look ridiculous if we try to do their dance or deploy their argot. The confidence that they mostly don't know they have, that is born of inexperience, is painful to see because it reminds us of when we had our own. So clueless! So thoughtless! So full of themselves! Poems seem to spill out of them. How we miss that fullness, that verve.

Experience teaches you that the world is not simply an unfolding architecture of knowledge, it is unfolding you too. Your voice will be broken over and again. You'll be formed as much by what cannot be resolved or understood. Early writing is clumsy, confident and adamant. Everything is subject matter because everything is new. Your thoughts are fresh. You haven't started bumping into yourself – *Am I saying that again?* Life darkens and fractures. Your experience, knowledge and awareness are richer but you falter. By now you will have done things that make you wonder if you know yourself at all. You'll have created little folds in your memory, necessary concealments which make yourself possible. There will be emergencies and times when you make a decision that could never be entirely right. You can find a reason for what you've done because there are so many words to choose from. You lose trust in language. You discover that there are things you don't want to know. You refuse to see what you're doing.

For years, I have been misquoting Rilke's advice:

Go into yourself. Search for the reason that bids you write; find out whether it is spreading out its roots in the deepest places of your heart . . .

Rainer Maria Rilke[11]

I remembered this as 'Go to the roots of the tree in your heart', which to me meant that you had first to find out what was in your heart, to feel it alive and growing, and then pursue its roots, to go underground and work with it there, below the level of narrative and anecdote, memory and 'what really happened', at the point of essential experience. Rilke's image is quite different. He seems to be saying that the reason you write could be found anywhere. The question is, has it taken root and in the right place, which is the deepest place in your heart, the hardest to reach, the most undisturbed?

My sense of how writing operates through the self encompasses both these ideas. I still like the notion of a tree in my heart (miraculous and forceful), the sensation of its branching and above all its roots. Rilke is right in that whatever leads to writing has to take root in the writer.

But if your language and ideas have never been uprooted, you will be in the same place, looking in the same direction, sounding as you did at twenty.

How did you find your voice? By breaking it – and by tracing the roots of what then grows back to my heart.

27. Solitude and its opposite

I think your early writing needed solitude, protection while you
realised what it was . . . So I hardly knew anything about it.

This book evolved out of a question that I could not answer.
Why did I write a memoir about music without mentioning
that I sang and had been in a band? The question took years
to form and, once it was in front of me, wouldn't go away. If
someone asked, I would say only that I was embarrassed. To
myself, that I was ashamed. Rather than push at the question,
I made my way behind it and there I was – worried about
being young or a woman among men or making a sound that
wasn't mine. I then had to make my way behind myself to what
anyone might recognise – the broader ground of presence and
power and voice.

This deep work depends on extended periods of solitude.
Every morning, I have to find my way back in and then, after a
few hours at my desk, I need to move away but stay within the
world I'm writing about, carrying whatever bit I'm working on
in my head as I do the other things required of that day. The
mornings when I wake up and realise that I will see no one fill
me with relief.

I write most easily in the early morning, having spoken to
no one and heard no news. I make a pot of tea and get started.
I'll wash, dress and eat a few hours later. After that, once I've

looked about me, I'll wander from room to room, unable to write again until things are tidy. There's a pile of clothes on a chair. There is little in the fridge. I should call my mother. Why hasn't my daughter called me? Is something wrong? My students are asking for help. Why have I not heard from my students? Plants are dying, dust is gathering. I have to respond and I have to work. I also need to be able to spend some days working in my head and appearing to do nothing. That's hard when you are observed. Who could take such so-called work seriously?

I need to be alone so as to let my ideas become words in their own time. My mind has to sustain a delicate connection with something as persistent as it is remote.

> It is precisely for feeling that one needs time and not thought. Thought is a flash of lightning, feeling is a ray from the most distant of stars.
>
> Marina Tsvetaeva[12]

When I'm not writing, I sense its pull. I can't hear what other people are saying or make space for other worlds. There's an impatience to get back to it and a resentment of all that stands in its way. I feel the weight of it, its gnawing nature, constantly.

There is also the solitude of being the only person who inhabits a book while it is being written. I am happily alone inside such a world for years at a time. If asked what I'm working on, I try to answer (*it's only polite*) and say too much because I feel immediately unconvinced. I don't want to talk about it and despise myself for doing so. I can come up with a line but it will have little to do with the true nature of the dark country and deep sea where I'm spending my days. My connection with this other world is never stable but, once established, it is primary and unquestioned. My doubts lie in my ability to realise it on the page, not in its existence. In this at least, I do not need the validation of others. More than that, I need there to be no one looking, asking or trying to follow. How fortunate I was to have a mother who understood before I did that my writing needed protection while I realised what it was, and who allowed me to experience a kind of solitude.

The work is difficult and unsettling. I have to stay still when I think I've found what I'm looking for and wait for it to form. I want to carry it, full of life, into my writing rather than just describe or record. Often I discover that it isn't what I expected it to be at all. I must dispense with what I've started to say and begin again. About half this book has been crossed out. (I spoke too soon.) It is in my solitude that its aspects have become clear.

—

Men have traditionally written about solitude with the confidence that comes from assuming that life will be taken care of while they're away. They climb mountains, wander hills, catch trains, board ships, set off into deserts and jungles and snow with the equilibrium that depends on having people at home who will look after each other in their absence. They are so secure in their presence that they assume it will continue to be felt in the household even as they go away. They will not lose their place.

Twenty years ago, I was given a prize that offered me a couple of months each year in the Swiss Alps. In the time I spent there,

I met only one male writer who arrived alone. All the women did. I sat in my sparsely furnished room, wondering whether to risk driving the car I'd been lent, with its failing brakes, down the mountain to buy some bread or if I was feeling brave enough to go into the bar alone or take myself up a mountain path, and I stayed at home. I didn't have the internet and needed to plan carefully which books to bring. I scoffed at those men with their 'trailing spouses' but I wasn't doing all that well without one. The more time I spent by myself, the harder it became to interact with other people. I created a routine of minor activities, achieving less and less each day because I had to work so hard to feel alright.

—

When the pandemic hit, I understood how carefully measured my solitude had been. I had relied on being able to control how far away I would be from people and for how long. I didn't feel as if time opened up because the space that time is supposed to offer collapsed. My thoughts kept reaching and flailing, which felt like perpetually forgetting what I was about to say. Time started to flail as well. The past had been uncoupled from a present that was refusing to form. I existed in speculation, using up my energies in perpetual adaptation as my mind relaxed and then remembered once more. It was exhausting.

Just before the first lockdown began, a friend came to stay. We spent the weekend doing the things we'd planned but with new consciousness and hesitation. We made a joke about it as we hugged when I picked her up from the station. Two days later, we didn't hug when I waved her off. In between, we walked, sat, ate and drank together, all the while talking about what was happening. We were both distracted by concern for our mothers, or friends who were alone or frail, and also by wondering what we had in our cupboards. We went into shops where people were behaving normally and wondered if we should take advantage of our advance information. Or was it that everyone else knew what we did and, like us, didn't want to be seen to take advantage of what was for now plentiful supply? We shared the superstitions and anecdotes that were already starting to do the rounds. We felt bonded in the way that people do if they were together when war was declared. We tried to talk about other things but always came back to the virus, our mothers and our cupboards.

When she left, I found it difficult to gauge how it felt to be alone now that I had no idea how long it would be for. If only she could stay and we could just keep talking about what was happening, I might be able to adjust. Unlike the solitude I contrived for myself, this was one I couldn't determine, let alone end.

I didn't write anything for weeks because most of my energy was spent on establishing ways to continue my university work and worrying about those I could no longer reach. What if my daughter, who lived abroad, was unwell? Or if my mother, who lived two hundred miles away and whose husband was approaching death, needed me? I was equally worried about those nearby. Had I given the virus to my ninety-year-old neighbour by taking him some milk? My mind ran up and down the same small track. I was listening to the news, check-ing my cupboards and calling my mother.

When I managed to stop working and took myself outside, the empty landscape seemed oddly tense. I looked up into the sky or out to sea and no longer felt an expansion of the self. Everywhere was empty now.

My desire for contact simplified. Conversations and messages were tender, direct and vital. I would not see my beloved for months. I woke up one morning and my phone was dead, I couldn't find my watch and the mirror was broken. I was well and truly cut off (at last!) but didn't have the courage to remain so. This was a state of emergency and I could not allow myself to be out of reach.

My body divided itself, as it does in times of stress, clean down the middle, and my left side, from top to toe, felt less alive. For once I felt no alarm because if I needed medical attention, it would be difficult to get. So I made a pact with my body. I would trust it for now.

Habits such as those of grief and anger were difficult to account for when no one was around and there had been no significant event. The constant feeling of being tugged at, of a towering list of things I had forgotten to do, turned out to form in my bloodstream. I learnt that I am in some ways my opposite – withholding where I thought I spilt and empty where I thought myself full.

—

Solitude can be achieved among people if you can pass unnoticed among them. The city where I was born, that I defend and love, where I cannot sleep and find it difficult to breathe, where I have to concentrate on keys and locks and

164

shadows, has given me much solitude. Before the year of lockdowns, I hadn't realised how much I depended on the city's sheer flow while moving through it, gathering static from its dense, intricate, inefficient, continuous activity. I need solitude but I know now that I form it out of its opposite: crowds and noise and the intrusion of strangers; interruption, diversion, abrasion, life.

28. Fuck quiet

You are in a large, crowded hall. The lights have been dimmed and the event has already started when in comes a woman who is in late middle age. She stands in a slant of unwelcome light and then flinches when the door makes a slight creak as she moves to close it. She grimaces as if to say to anyone who has turned their head *I know, I'm sorry.* There are empty chairs in the front row of the auditorium but she will not take one. She stands there until an usher indicates to her that she needs to sit down and directs her towards the front row. And so she sets out. She cannot seem to do this smoothly and efficiently. Why not? It's a simple matter of crossing a room. No, before she sets out she transforms herself into an apology. She hunches her shoulders and raises her hands as if to fend off attack. She embarks on a slow-motion scuttle, exaggerated creeping steps as if she needs to make sure we all know that she's taking as few steps as possible. When she reaches the seat, she sits straight down and makes no adjustment, however uncomfortable, other than to draw herself in.

By creeping like that, by becoming her own apology, she has invited us to receive her with contempt. *I am no longer viable but please let me stay. I will take up as little space as possible and you can laugh at me. I laugh at me. I despise myself and I invite you to despise me also. It will be good for you.* I used to watch such women and vow not to become them. I hadn't thought

166

about all the ways in which I was already creeping into rooms and embodying apology. Or how my writing crept and apologised at times.

The answer is not to become like those who march into that room and make not the slightest concession to where they are. They don't try to be quiet or signal apology but head straight for the front row and stand there choosing the best seat, take their time. Once settled they relax, spreading their legs and elbows. There's no point signalling your disapproval because they will not receive it.

I've watched women who refuse to creep and who move into such rooms with authority and calm. They take the time they need and I've learnt from them. Those who come in noisily and thoughtlessly because they have decided never to creep in again make me uncomfortable but they have taught me something too.

I've also seen women make a point of claiming space in ways that take from other women, take from an occasion and from everyone in the room. Each speaker has ten minutes but she takes forty. She speaks slowly as if each of her thoughts is delicious and we must watch her savour them. She is sure of the value of what she's saying. She looks straight at the audience, whom she does not appear to need. For years she had no audience but she will not be grateful now. There will be no jokes, anecdotes or asides or anything to signal that while she is speaking of serious things, she will also relieve us from the pressure of her intent. She won't be comical or cute and above all she will not creep.

The surface layer of my response is irritation. Her forty-minute monologue has thrown the whole event out of whack.

Those speaking after her feel hurried and the chairperson is in despair. The audience have been listening for long enough. They found her majestic but unrelenting. Even so, I prefer her to the woman who follows, who tries to help get things back on track by cutting her own time short, who flutters and apologises, and scatters jokes and anecdotes as if it's her job to clean the room of this seriousness, this weight. She's handed herself over to the situation and taken responsibility for making others comfortable even though it's not her job. Like the woman who took her time, she's just there to speak. This fluttering, scattering, joking, creeping woman is me.

Just below my irritation there is a pulsing anxiety. I'm willing the woman who is taking her time to look at her watch. The annoyance of my fellow panellists, the yawning man in the front row, the sweat breaking out on the face of the chairperson, are somehow my problems to fix. If a light bulb blows or water is spilt or someone faints in that warm and crowded hall, I feel I have to fix that too. There is this housework, this mother work, to be done but I can't do it because I'm sitting there on stage, trying not to be heard or seen while the woman talks on. I remember watching my daughter in a school play, her face pale with concentration as, barely perceptibly, she mouthed the words that belonged to everyone on the stage. She didn't know she was doing it.

For all my anxiety, what lasts is admiration. I wouldn't feel this if the woman taking her time had tried to persuade us of her right to do so. It was the fact that she didn't need to. She wasn't making a point. She valued what came from deep within herself but her conviction and investment lay in her ideas as *apart* from herself. What we thought of her was not the point.

29. The things I have wanted to say and the stories I will not tell

This is not a book of my stories. It is about the body and noise.

I do not want to insist on my truth but to pursue a voice that is truthful.

I want you to think with me.

I try to write with an awareness of what I do not know.

I do not know what I know.

There are things I have told strangers whom I've met in the dark that I will not tell you. I will not write them down. Why do I need so strongly to speak those words that I will offer them to a stranger? Why do I assume that this person of whom I know nothing will leave what I tell them there in the dark? Perhaps it doesn't matter what happens to these stories. They are free to go. What I need is to enter the dark and tell them to someone I will never see again. I can only write if I believe this is what I am doing.

My writing is shaped by the stories I will not tell.

I will not tell the stories that I do not want to be told.

There is pain that would only intensify by being shared. Not everything will be resolved by being spoken of. Words are not always a form of release.

Writing each part of this book has changed my mind about what the truth might be.

I have not arrived at a conclusion but at an answer in the form of what lies behind the question.

Each time I write, I am reconstruing the relationship between truth and lies in order better to tell the truth.

Or to convey the truth. Where words are refused, music can still enter. Sometimes you must sing what cannot be said.

30. Speechlessness

> I want to learn greater quiet, & force . . . Have I got the
> power needed if quiet is not to become insipid. These
> questions I will leave, for the moment, unanswered.
>
> Virginia Woolf[13]

The disappearing act of writing can only be achieved by having
been present in the first place. It begins in the relationship I
have with my subject. I have made contact with my subject but
nothing has been said.

The time before I find the words. The time between words. The
time spent testing and turning them over.

I am not interested in being able to say everything out loud.

When I don't have the words for something, I might have the
shape of it. Or the shape of an absence – something is present
that I haven't yet noticed.

The importance of emptiness (capacity) and stillness (concentration). I am using (not being) myself, leaving myself behind.
The aim is to feel movement through me. The endpoint is forgetting that I'm there.

I don't write towards a sense of catharsis so much as detail giving way. I suppose in myself. A simplification.

Writing might be a deferral of speech. In this, it might be used to suppress feeling.

I will not force an explanation.

Only I can give myself permission to speak – or not to speak. I cannot control being heard, listened to or understood.

If I silence myself, I want this to be an act of strength. I have chosen how I want to talk about these things. I do not want to discuss it.

I had to stop reading poems about my father's illness and death out loud. I cancelled all events because if I said the words, acute pain exploded in my right side. Even explaining the problem could make me cry. For most of my life I have felt compelled to speak (to explain, to reply) when it was expected of me. For once I was able to say that I couldn't.

Speechlessness isn't something I've left behind with a less assured self. I write to overcome my silenced self but also to achieve a condition of silence. I write myself into silence – for the joy of feeling that I no longer have to say anything at all.

Acknowledgements

Some of this draws on ideas first explored elsewhere. Thank you, Ace Records, BBC Radio 3 and 4, *The Believer*, The Folio Society, *London Review of Books*, Poetry Foundation, Poet in the City/King's Place Music Foundation, *New Statesman*. Thank you to my agents, Sarah Chalfant and Alba Ziegler-Bailey, and to all at Faber, especially my editors Alex Bowler and Emmie Francis, Kate Burton, Silvia Crompton, Paddy Fox and Anne Owen.

Notes

I

1 Friedrich Nietzsche (trans. R. J. Hollingdale), *Beyond Good and Evil*, Penguin Books, 1973

2 Horace (trans. W. G. Shepherd), 'Integer Vitae', in *The Complete Odes and Epodes*, Penguin Books, 1983

3 Edmund Gosse, *Father and Son: A Study of Two Temperaments* (1907), Penguin Books, 1989

4 Gosse, *Father and Son*

5 Letter from Emily Dickinson to Thomas Wentworth Higginson, August 1862. All Dickinson correspondence taken from Thomas H. Johnson (ed.), *Selected Letters of Emily Dickinson*, Belknap Press, 1986

6 This observation was made by Elizabeth Falsey of the Houghton Library at Harvard University, who kindly showed me the sampler in 2003

7 Letter from Emily Dickinson to Thomas Wentworth Higginson, August 1862

8 Denise Levertov, 'A Map of the Western Part of the County of Essex in England', in Donald Hall (ed.), *Contemporary American Poetry*, Penguin Books, 1972

9 Zdzisław Najder, *Joseph Conrad: A Life*, Camden House, 2007

II

1 T. S. Eliot, 'Portrait of a Lady' from *Prufrock and Other Observations* (1917) © Set Copyrights Limited 2015, in *The Poems of T. S. Eliot*, Volume I, Christopher Ricks and Jim McCue (eds), Faber & Faber, 2015

2 M. W. Croll, 'The Baroque Style in Prose' (1929), quoted by Elizabeth Bishop in a letter to Donald Stanford, 20th November 1933, in Elizabeth Bishop (ed. Robert Giroux), *One Art: The Selected Letters*, Chatto & Windus, 1994

3 Ivy Compton-Burnett quoted in Kay Dick, *Ivy & Stevie*, Gerald Duckworth and Company, 1971

4 Anni Albers, 'Work with Material', *Black Mountain College Bulletin*, 5, 1938

5 Thomas Mann (trans. Helen Lowe-Porter), 'A Weary Hour', in *Collected Stories*, Everyman's Press, 2001

6 Friedrich Nietzsche, 'The Parable of the Madman' (1882), in *The Gay Science*, trans. Walter Kaufmann, Random House, 1974

7 Dorothea Tanning, *Birthday and Beyond* exhibition brochure, Philadelphia Museum of Art, 2000

8 Ovid (trans. Mary M. Innes), *Metamorphoses*, Penguin Books, 1955

9 Thomas Bulfinch, *Myths of Greece and Rome* (compiled by Bryan Holme), Penguin Books, 1981

10 Allen Mandelbaum (trans.), *The Metamorphoses of Ovid*, Houghton Mifflin Harcourt Books, 1993

11 Bulfinch, *Myths of Greece and Rome*

12 Ovid/Innes, *Metamorphoses*

13 Ovid/Mandelbaum, *Metamorphoses*

14 Ovid/Innes, *Metamorphoses*

15 Ovid/Innes, *Metamorphoses*

16 'Comme le développement de cristaux: une volonté de formation, et une impossibilité de se former autrement que *d'une manière*.' Francis Ponge (trans. Margaret Guiton), 'Faune et Flore', in *Selected Poems*, Wake Forest University Press, 1994

17 Sylvia Plath to Aurelia Schober Plath, 21 April 1956, in Peter K. Steinberg and Karen V. Kukil (eds), *The Letters of Sylvia Plath, Volume I: 1940–1956*, Faber & Faber, 2017

18 Plath, 29 April 1956

19 H.D. (ed. Norman Holmes Pearson and Michael King), *End to Torment: A Memoir of Ezra Pound by H.D.*, Carcanet New Press, 1980

III

1 Elizabeth Bishop, 'The Bight', in *Complete Poems*, Farrar Straus and Giroux, 1983
2 Shakespeare, *King Lear*, III ii and *Twelfth Night*, V i
3 Tillie Olsen, *Silences*, Virago, 1980
4 Letter from Emily Dickinson to Elizabeth Holland, May 1866
5 Introduction to Emily Dickinson (ed. Thomas H. Johnson), in *The Complete Poems*, Faber & Faber, 1976
6 Letter from Emily Dickinson to Thomas Wentworth Higginson, 25 April 1862
7 Letter from Emily Dickinson to Abiah Root, late 1850
8 Emily Dickinson, quoted in a letter from Thomas Wentworth Higginson to Mary Channing, 16 August 1870
9 Dickinson, in a letter from Thomas Wentworth Higginson, August 1870
10 Randall Jarrell, 'The Obscurity of the Poet', in *Poetry and the Age*, Farrar, Straus and Giroux, 1953
11 Rainer Maria Rilke (trans. M. D. Herter Norton), *Letters to a Young Poet*, W. W. Norton, 1993
12 Marina Tsvetaeva quoted in Tillie Olson, *Silences*, op. cit.
13 Diary entry, 30th July 1925, in Virginia Woolf, *A Writer's Diary: Being Extracts from the Diary of Virginia Woolf*, (1953), Harvest Books, 2003